God's
Ten Commandments
Yesterday
Today
Forever

GOD'S
TEN COMMANDMENTS
YESTERDAY
TODAY
FOREVER

REV. DR. ADV.
FRANCIS NIGEL LEE
LL.B., D.JUR., D.C.L., PH.D., TH.D.

Nordskog
Publishing Inc.
Ventura, California

GOD'S TEN COMMANDMENTS: YESTERDAY, TODAY, FOREVER

PUBLISHED BY

© 2007 by Francis Nigel Lee

Intenational Standard Book Number: 978-0-9796736-2-7

Library of Congress Control Number: 2007930763

Unless otherwise indicated, Scripture quotations are
translated from the original languages by
Dr. Francis Nigel Lee.

Theology Editor: Rev. Christopher Hoops
Cover: Tim Bepler, Bepler Design
Manuscript Editing: Mark Kakkuri
Proofing: Kimberley Winters
Editing & Book Design: Desta Garrett, www.dg-ink.net

For Information & Ordering:
NORDSKOG PUBLISHING, INC.
2716 Sailor Avenue, Ventura, CA 93001
1-805-642-2070 • 1-805-276-5129
www.nordskogpublishinginc.com

Dr. Lee authored the gist of this book in an extended article published in
Blue Banner Faith & Life, Vol. 29:1, 1974 (Beaver Falls, Pennsylvania, U.S.A.).
While Scholar-in-Residence at Christian Studies Center in Memphis,
Tennessee, the material, in abridged form, appeared in the booklet, *Ten
Commandments Today!* (The Lord's Day Observance Society, London, 1976).
    A Table Illustration of "God's Eternal Moral Law" (pages 82–83), is
reworked from the author's 1966 Th.D. thesis, *The Covenantal Sabbath*.

Christian Small Publishers Association

Dedication

To Chief Justice Roy S. Moore of Alabama,
after the wretched removal by quasi-legal tyranny
of his monument of the Ten Commandments
from the Alabama State Supreme
Court Building's Rotunda
on that "Day of Infamy," August 27, 2003.

—*Francis Nigel Lee*

Contents

~

ILLUSTRATIONS

~

Dr. Francis Nigel Lee is a man deeply devoted to God. His extensive research and study demonstrates the truth found in Ecclesiastes 12:13, that the fear of God and His Holy Law is what man is all about. Our society, and indeed our civilization, would greatly benefit by a better understanding of the intricate design of God for His creation. Sir William Blackstone in his *Commentaries on the Laws of England* said it most explicitly, when he stated:

Man considered as a creature,
must necessarily be subject to the laws of his Creator,
for he is entirely a dependent being.

I am happy to commend to your reading Dr. Lee's work *God's Ten Commandments: Yesterday, Today, Forever.*

Honorable Roy S. Moore

Former Chief Justice, Alabama Supreme Court
President, Foundation for Moral Law, Inc.

FORMER CHIEF JUSTICE ROY MOORE
WITH PUBLISHERS, GERALD AND GAIL NORDSKOG

About Dr. Francis Nigel Lee
& Judge Roy Moore

The Old Testament states & the New Testament affirms!

That He might make you know that
man shall not live by bread alone;
but man lives by every word that proceeds
from the mouth of the LORD. (Deuteronomy 8:3b, NKJV)

But Jesus answered him saying,
"It is written, Man shall not live by bread alone,
but by every word of God." (Luke 4:4, NKJV)

*T*HIS book is about God telling mankind to live by His Word, His Laws, in every age, for all peoples, from the beginning of creation to the end of time and for eternity.

As publisher I am pleased that my friend, Dr. Francis Nigel Lee, provided his manuscript for the publishing of this important work, showing throughout a scholarly *rightly-dividing* of the Word of Truth with more than ample Holy Scripture references, that The Ten Commandments (summarizing all of God's Law) are for Yesterday, and for Today, and Forever.

In 1989, I first met Dr. Lee through a friend and member (Mr. Frank Gauna) of my Southern California Constitution Education Committee, founded prior to the 1987 Bicentennial of the U.S. Constitution. Dr. Lee flew from Australia to America for several speaking engagements including our SCCEC all-day seminar the weekend prior to Thanksgiving in Chatsworth, California. He spoke on the subject of "Communists More Religious Than Christians!" (also recorded in his book *Adventures with God*, page 136), and we soon became life-long (but primarily distant) friends.

Then again in 1997 (page 175 of his book), Dr. Lee went on a speaking tour in the U.S.A. and we were privileged to host him at our George Washington/ Patrick Henry Supper Club in Ventura, California, where he spoke about "Restoring the U.S.'s Common Law" and on "The American War between the States (Civil War)."

That same weekend, my wife Gail and I invited Dr. Lee to our Sunday evening home Bible class where he gave the most interesting and passionate talk about his life with Christ, and his witnessing over some period of time to his dad's murderer while the man was in a Republic of South Africa jail and leading him to Jesus Christ. Dr. Lee had demonstrated forgiveness and great compassion in showing the love of the Lord (also recorded in his autobiography *Adventures with God* starting at page 121).

Dr. Lee was born in England, grew up in South Africa, emigrated to the U.S.A. and eventually settled permanently *down under* in Australia. He has preached well over 3000 sermons in Afrikaans and English, written well over 500 published articles, and has nearly 200 books he has authored in print, totaling well over 30,000 pages of text (see partial list on pages 85–90).

This book is dedicated by Nigel Lee to the honor of former Alabama Chief Justice Roy Moore (now known as "The Ten Commandments Judge"), for his courageous stance in upholding The Ten Commandments. Judge Moore has shown himself to be a man of valor, integrity, and comprehensive familiarity with the original Constitutional principles, and a stalwart defender of religious liberty.

He is a West Point graduate and served our country as a U.S. Army Company Commander in Vietnam before earning a Juris Doctor degree from the University of Alabama Law School. A highly respected Constitutional scholar, Judge Moore served as the Chief Justice of the Supreme Court in Alabama from 2001 until he was removed from office for daring to refuse a liberal judge's unconstitutional court order to remove a Ten Commandments monument from the State Supreme Court building. This was a historic and heroic stand for God's Law, The Ten Commandments.

A tireless defender of individual liberties, Judge Moore has been honored by at least three states and dozens of civic organizations, including "Christian Statesman of the Year" award, "Bill of Rights" award, and the "God and Country" award. Judge Moore initially was thrust into the national spotlight in 1997 when he held his ground against a court order demanding that he remove a tablet of The Ten Commandments, which he had carved by hand and hung on the wall alongside his court bench in Etowah County, Alabama. Eventually this led to his placement of the famous 5280-pound Ten Commandments monument in 2001, and his stance not to cave in to pressure from those who brazenly reject God's Law as the moral foundation of our legal system.

My wife, Gail, and I had a wonderful opportunity to meet Judge Roy Moore (and have our picture taken with him) at the Celebration of Justice Banquet of the Pacific Justice Institute (PJI) founded by Brad Dacus at a gala in Orange County, California, in 2005, when Judge Moore was the honoree and the keynote speaker. We are thrilled that Dr. Nigel Lee has dedicated this book to Judge Roy Moore, both gentlemen being distinguished and faithful and courageous servants of the Lord.

—Gerald Christian Nordskog
Ventura, California, USA

About the Author

$\mathcal{D}$R. Francis Nigel Lee was an Advocate or Barrister (Trial Lawyer) of the Supreme Court of South Africa, before becoming a minister and then pastoring congregations of the Presbyterian Church in America (PCA) in Mississippi and Florida. He was also Professor of Philosophy at Shelton College in New Jersey; Scholar in Residence at the Christian Studies Center in Memphis, Tennessee; Academic Dean of Graham Bible College in Bristol, Tennessee; and then, for twenty years, Professor of Theology

 and Church History at the Queensland Presbyterian Theological College in Australia where he now lives in retirement with his wife and two daughters.

THE TEN COMMANDMENTS

Exodus 20:1–17

(Translation by F. N. Lee)

God spoke all these words, saying:

I AM the LORD your God, Who brought you out of the land of Egypt, out of the house of slavery.

1 *You shall have no other gods before Me.*

2 *You shall not make for yourself any engraved image or any likeness of anything that is in Heaven above, or that is in the Earth beneath, or that is in the water under the Earth; you shall not bow yourself down to them nor serve them: for I the LORD your God am a jealous God, punishing the iniquity of the fathers in the children, to the third and fourth generations of those that hate Me; but showing mercy to thousands of those who love Me and who keep My Commandments.*

3 *You shall not take the Name of the LORD your God in vain; for the LORD will not hold him guiltless who takes His Name in vain.*

4 *Remember the Sabbath Day, to keep it holy. Six days you shall labor, and do all your work; but the seventh day is the Sabbath of the* LORD *our God: on it you shall not do any work, you, nor your son, nor your daughter, your male employee or your female employee, nor your domestic animals, nor your visitor within your city-gates. For in six days the* LORD *made Heaven and Earth, the sea and all that is in them, and rested the seventh day. Therefore the* LORD *blessed the sabbath day and hallowed it.*

5 *Honor your father and your mother, so that your days may be long in the land which the* LORD *your God gives you.*

6 *You shall not murder.*

7 *You shall not commit adultery.*

8 *You shall not steal.*

9 *You shall not bear false witness against your neighbor.*

10 *You shall not covet your neighbor's house; you shall not covet your neighbor's wife, nor his male employee, nor his female employee, nor his ox nor his donkey nor anything that is your neighbor's.*

Sketch of the Tablets of the Law

Introduction

God gave man Ten Commandments. Every one of them is vital, in all ages. For only by observing them can man live a full life each week, maintain a happy marriage, and function well in his home, his job, and even in the world internationally.

God Himself is the Root of the Moral Law, and perfectly reflects it. Salvation was never by the works of the Law. For even before the fall, man was to keep it out of gratitude for God's great grace. Unfallen man kept the whole Decalogue. The Sabbath, Marriage, the Forbidden Fruit, and the Tree of Life all reveal it.

When man broke God's Law, he degenerated more and more—from the Fall to the Flood. The Patriarchs kept it, and the Prophets called man back to keep it. So, too, should we.

Christ never broke it. He said He had not come to destroy but to finish building the Law, and that not one jot or tittle of it would ever fail until heaven and earth themselves pass away (Matthew 5:17–18).

Also, subsequently, all His Apostles taught it. So, too, did the Early Church Fathers, King Alfred, Luther, Calvin, and even the great Jurist Sir William Blackstone. It is the very basis of the United States of America, and also of every other Common Law nation in the world.

True Christians love to Keep God's Law. They shall always do so in Heaven. But all unsaved Law-breakers, will end up in Hell.

Re-promulgation and Re-announcement of God's Law

"For the Primordial Law was given to Adam and Eve in Paradise, as the womb of all the precepts of God. . . . Before the Law of Moses written on tablets of stone. . . . There was an unwritten Law which habitually was understood 'naturally' and which was habitually kept by the Fathers."

Tertullian of Charthage, 200 A.D.

Illustration adapted from NIV Discoverer's Bible.
Copyright The Holy Bible, New International Version ® 1973, 1978, 1984
by International Bible Society, 2002 by the Zondervan Corporation.
Used by permission of Zondervan.

2

God's Ten Commandments: Yesterday, Today, Forever!

"*A*LL their life was spent not in laws, statutes or rules—but according to their own free will and pleasure. They rose out of their beds when they thought good. They did eat, drink, labor, sleep, when they had a mind to it and were disposed to it. . . . In all their rule and strictest land to their order, there was but this one clause to be observed: Do whatever you wish!"[1]

Thus wrote the Renaissance humanist Rabelais of his own ideal for a model society. There, "all the nuns are beautiful." There, chastity, contentment, and obedience are not praised. There, all may cohabit indiscriminately, become plutocrats, and live licentiously.

This represents the very epitome of Antinomianism, or disregard for God's Law. Such advocates what He never requires, and requires what He never advocates.

3

From time to time, to a lesser extent, however, such tendencies have been found on the fringes and even within the Christian Church. They were particularly prominent among wildcat heresies before, during, and after the sixteenth century, when some went and murdered their religious opponents (breaking God's Sixth Commandment) and others practiced polygamy and community of property (breaking God's Seventh and Eighth Commandments).[2]

Less extreme examples of this loose attitude toward the Ten Commandments, or the Decalogue, are found also among modern Christians. Sadly, one frequently encounters in the worship of some evangelicals a total liturgical ignoring of the Decalogue and a misunderstanding of the Christian's position in relation to it. The heretical hymn "Free from the Law, O happy condition!" illustrates this.

Sadder still are theological liberals who support revolutionary action, and libertines and sexual perverts who demand freedom from all legal strictures. And, saddest yet, traces of this disregard for God's most holy Law are found in some groups that claim to be "reformational" and even "law-oriented."

I do not intend here to undertake a detailed analysis of how people—consciously or unconsciously—undermine the Decalogue in general or the Sabbath in particular.[3] Undermining either the Decalogue or the

Sabbath betrays the amateur, naïve, and untheological influence of apostate religion and is the basic motive of Antinomianism—at least at a secondary or tertiary level.

Rather I present the view of the infallible written Word of God—the sixty-six-book Bible, the final rule for all matters of faith and conduct (Second Timothy 3:16–17: cf. First Timothy 5:18; Luke 10:7; First Peter 1:10–12, 23–25; Second Peter 1:19–21, 3:15–16). It clearly teaches that all men, of all religions, of all cultures, and for all time, are obligated to follow the Ten Commandments. So, in the words of Romans 4:3, what does Scripture say?

Salvation Was Never by the Works of the Law

*M*AN was never required to work for his salvation, not even before the Fall.[4] Only the undeserved favor (or "grace") of God alone first created and subsequently preserved man (Luke 2:40, 3:23-38: cf. Revelation 4:11).

Although God required unfallen man to keep His Commandments, man's obedience was not the meritorious ground of his obtaining of everlasting life. To the contrary, man's obedience was an expression of gratitude—part of his "reasonable service" (Romans 12:1) and his "pure religion and undefiled" (James 1:26-27)—to Almighty God. Obedience reflected man's thankfulness to the Lord for already having given him (losable) everlasting life (Ephesians 1:4-7, 2:8-10, 4:17-32, esp. vv. 22-24).

The everlasting life that God originally endowed to Adam could be lost, and was lost, as a result of his avoidable fall. Adam did not lose it, however, because he did not sufficiently earn merit with God. Scripture specifically declares that Adam lost everlasting life by disobeying God—eating the forbidden fruit of the tree of the knowledge of good and evil (Genesis 2:17, 3:3, 11, 17: cf. Philippians 3:19).

God Is the Root
of the Decalogue

SCRIPTURE says that God Himself is the Root of the Ten Commandments and that He created unfallen Law-abiding man as His Own image.

God's covenant, broken by Adam, presupposed the Ten Commandments (Hosea 6:7-10). The people of the antediluvian era all knew the Decalogue. And the patriarchs of ancient Israel kept God's Law long before the time of Moses.

The Decalogue was merely repromulgated on Mount Sinai. Christ revealed God's Law in His person, and enjoined it to His disciples. The New Testament Church kept all Ten Commandments. And, as they became Christianized, so also did all Western countries. God's children will always keep the Decalogue, even on the New Earth, unlike the devil and his hellish disciples.

God Himself is free from laws (*legibus solutus*). Nevertheless, as Calvin correctly points out, God is not capricious (*non exlex*).[5] The Law, far from being contrary to God (*contra Deum*), is, in every respect, in harmony with His nature (*secundum Deum*). It is a revelation of His own righteous goodness.

God created man as His image, thus reflecting something of God's own glory, albeit in a creaturely way (Genesis 1:26-28: cf. Second Corinthians 3:3-18, esp. v. 7). Likewise, God's Law reflects His own essential righteousness, His communicable "law-full-ness."

Various kinds of laws and norms, such as those found within the disciplines of mathematics, physics, and ethics (Job 28:26, 38:1-11, esp. v. 10; Psalms 119:89-91, 148:6; & Romans 7:26), all reveal[6] that God Himself is essentially a God of law and order (First Corinthians 14:26-40).

The Moral Laws of God, as expressed in the Ten Commandments, are all-embracing in their scope. In all ages, they are central for man as the very image of God; and they root in the very heart of God Himself. He is "the only true God" (John 17:3: cf. the First Commandment in Exodus 20:3). He "is Spirit" (John 4:24: cf. the Second Commandment in Exodus 20: 4-6). He "swears by Himself" (Hebrews 6:13: cf. the Third Commandment in Exodus 20:7). He "has entered into His rest." (Hebrews 4:3-4; Genesis 2:2-3:

cf. the Fourth Commandment in Exodus 20:8–11).

He is also "our Father Who is in Heaven" (Matthew 6:9: cf. the Fifth Commandment in Exodus 20:12). He is "the living God" (Acts 14:15: cf. the Sixth Commandment in Exodus 20:13). He is "pure" (First John 3:1: cf. the Seventh Commandment in Exodus 20:14). He is "the Giver of every good gift" (James 1:17: cf. the Eighth Commandment in Exodus 20:15). He "cannot lie" (Hebrews 6:18; Titus 1:2: cf. the Ninth Commandment in Exodus 20:16). And He is a jealous God (Exodus 20:5: cf. the Tenth Commandment in Exodus 20:17). All in all, He is the very Source of the Moral Law—and the "righteous Father" (John 17:25).

Unfallen Man
and the
Decalogue

$\mathcal{G}$OD created unfallen man as His Own image. While still in his state of rectitude, unfallen man imaged the communicable and the actually communicated righteousness of God Himself (Genesis 1:26–28; Ecclesiastes 7:29; Ephesians 4:23–24; Colossians 3:10).

Of course, unfallen man did this in only a reflective and creaturely way. Therefore, the substance of the Ten Commandments (in essence if not in form)[7] was stamped on the heart of the unfallen Adam even from the time of his creation.

About a century ago, Dr. Abraham Kuyper, the great theologian and Christian Prime Minister of the Netherlands, was asked: "Did Adam know the Ten Commandments?" Kuyper's answer: "Yes and no! Adam could not recite the Ten Commandments; but he had them written in his heart. That is to say, he thoroughly knew their moral significance even in the details."[8]

The Apostle Paul tells us that even unsaved and ignorant Gentiles have "the work of the Law written in their hearts, their consciences also bearing witness" (Romans 2:15). As such, even the Heathen are created as the image of God in the broader sense of the word (Genesis 5:1-3, 9:1-6; James 3:9).

They have some consciousness (however dim) of the Ten Commandments preserved as a remnant in their hearts by the continued operation of God's non-saving or common grace in spite of the fall.[9] Hence, it seems the Ten Commandments must have been written on the heart of their ancestor Adam. Further evidence for this comes from the fact that God also established His Covenant with the unfallen Adam and in him with all his descendants (Hosea 6:7-11).[10] Positively, this required man's execution of the Dominion Charter —*sometimes called the Cultural Mandate* (Genesis 1:28), and its accompanying institutions of Marriage and the weekly Sabbath (Genesis 1:26-2:3). All three imply the Ten Commandments.

Negatively, the Covenant required man to avoid eating of the tree of knowledge of good and evil (Genesis 2:17, 3:3-6, 3:11, & 3:17). This implied keeping the Ten Commandments.

Ultimately, man's keeping of this Covenant would have been rewarded with the gift of unlosable ever-

lasting life in its cosmos-embracing scope. This was
• foreshadowed by the tree of life (Genesis 2:9, 3:22: cf.
Revelation 2:7, & 22:14).

It further implies Adam's knowledge of the Covenant
as well as the necessity of his and his descendants' perpetual observance of the Ten Commandments. The
Dominion Charter, the weekly Sabbath, Marriage,
the tree of the knowledge of good and evil, and the
tree of life—presuppose the essence of the Ten
Commandments. They all provide additional conclu-
sive evidence that Adam—the forefather and federal
head of all people of all races and all religions—himself received and knew and was required to live by the
principles of the Decalogue.

Man was to execute the Dominion Charter—which
also implies the Ten Commandments and vice versa—
to the glory of the one, true, Triune God alone (Genesis
1:26; Psalm 8:1-9: cf. the First Commandment). Yet
• man was to subdue creation only, not the Creator
(which is sin). The latter, however, is sinfully attempted •
when men try to depict God (Genesis 1:28; & John
4:24: cf. the Second Commandment).

By subduing the Earth for God, Adam glorified His
name by subduing the Earth for His sake (Genesis
1:26-2:3; Psalm 8:1-9: cf. the Third Commandment).
• Further, after dominating and subduing the Earth in
six-day cycles of labor, Adam was to rest every Sabbath

(Genesis 1:28–2:3, & Hebrews 4:4–11: cf. the Fourth Commandment). This is what the great Polish Reformer John Laski believed;[11] and so, too, the great Dutch Statesman and Theologian Dr. Abraham Kuyper Sr.[12]

By laboring and resting, Adam honored his Heavenly Father (Genesis 1:28; & Psalm 8: cf. the Fifth Commandment). And in the exercise of his dominion, Adam was to preserve and to protect life (Genesis 1:28, 2:19–20, 7:1–3, 9:1–15: cf. the Sixth Commandment).

To be able to subdue the whole Earth, it was necessary for Adam to marry and to raise children—to help him to do this (Genesis 1:26–28, 2:18–25: cf. the Seventh Commandment). This enjoined multiplication and expansion of mankind, necessitated the institution of private property (Genesis 1:28, 2:24, 4:3–5: cf. the Eighth Commandment).

Adam was to view God's Word as truthful, obey it, and subdue the Earth (Genesis 1:28–31: cf. the Ninth Commandment). He was to enjoy all that God had given him, but he was not to desire God's Own private property by doing what God forbade him do—eating of the tree of the knowledge of good and evil (Genesis 2:16–17, & 3:6ff.: cf. the Tenth Commandment).

The Sabbath Reveals
the Decalogue

THE weekly Sabbath and its rest clearly reveals the Decalogue and complements the Dominion Charter and its required labor. The Sabbath intimately relates to the whole of the Moral Law. God, the Creator of Heaven and Earth, instituted it (Genesis 2:1-3: cf. the First Commandment). The Sabbath provides a special, though not an exclusive day, on which to worship God each week (Genesis 2:1-3; Exodus 20:4-11; Ezekiel 20:11-17: cf. the Second Commandment), and is sanctified by God under oath (Hebrews 3:11, & 4:4-5: cf. the Third Commandment). Further, the Sabbath prophesies everlasting rest (Hebrews 4:4-11; & Genesis 2:1-3: cf. the Fourth Commandment).

Observing the Sabbath respects God's authority (Ezekiel 20:10-14; & Exodus 20:8-11: cf. the Fifth Commandment) and predicts eternal life (Hebrews

4:4–11: cf. the Sixth Commandment). A man and wife together observing the Sabbath promotes their joint loyalty towards God and hence toward one another (Exodus 20:8–11; Deuteronomy 5:12–16; Leviticus 19:29–30: cf. the Seventh Commandment, thus Martin Luther).[13]

Observing the Sabbath regulates honest labor (Genesis 1:28–2:3: cf. the Eighth Commandment, and see also footnote 11), and bears out the true witnesses to God's promise of life (Genesis 1:28–2:3; Hosea 6:7; Genesis 2:9, 3:22; Psalm 95:11; Hebrews 4:1–11: cf. the Ninth Commandment). And its regular observance increases man's desire for the life to come. (See the previously cited texts and Revelation 14:12–13 [per contra vv. 9–11]: cf. the Tenth Commandment).

Marriage
Presupposes the
Decalogue

ARRIAGE, as an integral part of the Dominion Charter, also presupposes the Ten Commandments. It also illustrates the relationship of the divine Christ to the Christian Church, His obedient bride (Genesis 1:28; Ephesians 5:23: cf. the First Commandment). Marriage points to the spirituality of God Himself (Genesis 1:28; Ephesians 5:25–32; First Corinthians 7:14; Luke 1:15: cf. the Second Commandment). It honors God's Name (Genesis 1:26–28, 2:18–23, 3:20–22; Ephesians 3:14–15; Exodus 3:13ff., 4:20–26: cf. the Third Commandment). Indeed, marriage constantly reminds us of the idea of the everlasting Sabbath Rest (Ruth 3:1; Psalm 95:11; Hebrews 4:1–11; Genesis 1:26–2:3: cf. the Fourth Commandment).

Marriage results in the birth of children who are

to honor their parents (Genesis 1:26-28; Proverbs 1:8, 4:1-4: cf. the Fifth Commandment). It reproduces life (Genesis 1:26-28, 2:24-25, 3:15-20, & 4:1-2ff.: cf. the Sixth Commandment), and involves an exclusive relationship between two partners of the opposite sex (Genesis 2:24-25; Matthew 19:4-8: cf. the Seventh Commandment). Marriage also results in the establishment of a separate home and separate private property (Genesis 2:24, 4:3-4, & chaps. 30-31: cf. the Eighth Commandment), and involves truthfulness in mutual words (Ruth 4:9-11: cf. the Ninth Commandment). Marriage is also designed to combat covetousness (Exodus 20:17; First Thessalonians 4:4-5: cf. the Tenth Commandment).

The Forbidden Fruit
and the
Decalogue

$\mathcal{G}$od's prohibition of man eating of the fruit of the tree of the knowledge of good and evil, also presupposed the Ten Commandments. The prohibition, a test for man, was added only after God engraved the inherent Moral Law on our forefather Adam's heart at the beginning, and only after God audibly communicated to Adam the Dominion Charter (with all its implications re the Decalogue). Yet the test prohibition in every sense presupposed and reflected that Law which had already been revealed to Adam.

So the one and only true Triune God promulgated the prohibition to man (Genesis 2:16–17: cf. the First Commandment). And God communicated it to man directly (Genesis 2:16–17, & 3:11, 17: cf. the Second Commandment).

Breaching God's prohibition resulted in a solemn sanction or penalty for Adam and for his descendants (Genesis 3:11, 17; & Exodus 20:7: cf. the Third Commandment)—(everlasting) death. This implied the opposite reward for keeping the Commandment—everlasting life, also known as everlasting rest with God (Genesis 2:17, 3:22, 2:1-3; Hebrews 4:1-11: cf. the Fourth Commandment).

God required that man respect his authority in this matter (Genesis 2:16-17, 3:3, 11, 17; Romans 5:12-19: cf. the Fifth Commandment) and threatened death for disobedience (Genesis 2:17: cf. the Sixth Commandment). Breaching God's Commandment brought disunity between man and wife, and shame in their nakedness (Genesis 3:3-16: cf. the Seventh Commandment).

God's prohibition warned against the theft involved in its transgression (Genesis 2:17, 3:3-11: cf. the Eighth Commandment), and the violation involved accepting false witness about it from the devil (Genesis 3:3-5; John 8:44: cf. the Ninth Commandment). The covetousness of desiring the forbidden fruit immediately brought tragic consequences (Genesis 3:3-6; James 1:14-15: cf. the Tenth Commandment).

Incidentally, man's sin consisted not in studying this God-given tree and the Ten Commandments it represented; this he was required to do (Genesis

2:9, 17, 3:3; Psalms 1:2, 119:97, 100). Rather, man's sin consisted in disobeying God's Law (First John 3:4) by eating of the forbidden fruit (Genesis 3:11-17)—instead of subjecting himself to the revealed Law of God (Romans 8:7).

In this way, man became a law unto himself. He ignored what he had known was right in God's eyes and he did what he erroneously thought was right in his own eyes (Deuteronomy 12:8; Judges 17:6, 21:25).

He tried to ascertain or "know good and evil" apart from submitting to the clearly revealed will of God. Thus, man made a god out of himself and perverted his ideas of right and wrong (Genesis 3:5, 22).

In doing so, man attempted to restructure the essence of the Decalogue implied in the prohibition of eating from the forbidden tree. This disobedience to God's infallible Word is exactly what Antinomians or Law-haters do today.

The Tree of Life
Presupposes the
Decalogue

HE tree of life, foreshadowing man's ultimate reward, presupposed the Ten Commandments. For it pointed to the one true God (Genesis 2:9: cf. the First Commandment). It could be partaken of only in the appropriate way (Genesis 3:22; Revelation 2:7: cf. the Second Commandment). It somehow revealed God's Name (Genesis 3:22; Revelation 2:7, 17, 3:12: cf. the Third Commandment) and signified and sealed man's inheritance of unlosable everlasting life, that is, his Everlasting Sabbath Rest (Genesis 2:9, 3:22; Hebrews 4:1-11: cf. the Fourth Commandment).

The tree of life also pointed to a long life for obeying the Heavenly Father (Proverbs 3:1, 9, 11–18; Exodus 20:12: cf. the Fifth Commandment) and is the reward of the righteous who save souls from death (Proverbs 11:30; Revelation 22:2: cf. the Sixth Commandment).

It promoted the inheritance of everlasting life to both husband and wife together (Genesis 3:22; First Peter 3:7: cf. the Seventh Commandment). Unfallen man was invited to lay hold of it, but unregenerate fallen man has no right to possess it (Proverbs 3:18; Genesis 3:22: cf. the Eighth Commandment). "A wholesome tongue is a tree of life; but perverseness therein is a breach in the spirit" (Proverbs 15:4: cf. the Ninth Commandment). And when legitimate desire (as opposed to covetousness) is satisfied, it is a tree of life (Proverbs 13:12: cf. the Tenth Commandment). Indeed, "blessed are those that do His Commandments, so that they may have right to the tree of life!" (Revelation 22:14).

Hence, as the *Westminster Larger Catechism* declares, the first man and woman had "the Law of God written in their hearts, and power to fulfill it, with dominion over the creatures" (Q. 17). It adds that God "placed man in Paradise—appointing him to dress it; giving him liberty to eat of the fruit of the Earth; putting the creatures under his dominion, and ordaining Marriage for his help . . . ; instituting the Sabbath; [and] entering into a Covenant of Life with him—upon condition of personal, perfect, and perpetual obedience" (Q. 20).

In "ordaining Marriage for his help," God gave Adam and his entire posterity the substance of the Seventh Commandment (Q. 137ff.). In giving man "liberty to eat of the fruit of the Earth" and in "putting the creatures under his dominion," God enjoined the positive observance of the substance of the Sixth Commandment (Qs. 99 & 134ff.). And in placing man in "Paradise [and] appointing him to dress it," as well as in "instituting the Sabbath," God required man to keep the Eighth and Fourth commandments (Q. 117ff.).

The *Westminster Larger Catechism* clearly understands Scripture to teach that keeping the Ten Commandments requires man to subdue the entire Earth, keep the Sabbath, celebrate marriage, etc. All of this, man is to do entirely and utterly to the glory of God (First Corinthians 10:31).

According to Jesus, Adam knew the substance of the Seventh Commandment (Matthew 19:4–6). And, according to the writer of Hebrews, Adam was to observe the weekly Sabbath (Hebrews 4:3–11: cf. 6:7–8, 10:25, 11:1–4). That foreshadowed Adam's ultimate entry alongside God into what the great Puritan Richard Baxter, in the title of his famous book, called *The Saints' Everlasting Rest*. Hence, as Baxter also pointed out, we, too, (like Adam and Eve) are to use our Sabbaths as steps to Heaven, until we have arrived there.

So, as the great Westminster Assembly Commissioner John Lightfoot insisted: "Adam heard as much in the garden as Israel did at Sinai, but only in fewer words and without thunder."[14] Indeed, as the great Scottish Theologians Fisher and M'Crie and the American Scholar Louis Berkhof implied[15]—by eating of the forbidden fruit, Adam broke all Ten of God's Commandments all at once.[16]

Luther and Calvin
on
Adam's Decalogue

*I*N his Second Dispute against the Antinomians,[17] Luther stated: "The Ten Commandments are not of Moses. Nor did God give them first to him. On the contrary, the Decalogue belongs to the whole World. It was written and engraved in the minds of all human beings from the beginning of the World. . . . Later on, since men had finally come to the point of caring neither for God nor for men, God was compelled to renew their laws through Moses and, after writing them with His fingers on tablets [of stone], to place them before our eyes in order to present to us what we were before the fall of Adam and what someday we are to be in Christ."

Luther also accurately translated Hosea 6:7–10 regarding the later Israelites and Gileadites that "they, like Adam, transgressed the Covenant. . . . Gilead is a city full of idolatry. . . . Like a troop of robbers . . . they murder on the road. . . . There is whoredom."[18] Luther believed that when Adam sinned, he became an idolater and a robber and a murderer and a whore-monger—and thus transgressed the Second and the Eighth and the Sixth and the Seventh etc., of the Ten Commandments.

"The Law of Nature," explains Luther,[19] "is the Ten Commandments. It is written in the heart of every human being by creation. It was clearly and compre-hensively put on Mount Sinai. . . . It does not come from men, but is a created Law to which everyone who hears it cannot but consent."

Calvin, the genius of Geneva, saw it as "evident that the Law of God which we call 'Moral'—is nothing else than the testimony of Natural Law and of that conscience which God has engraven on the minds of men. . . . The whole of this equity of which we now speak, is prescribed in it. Hence—it alone ought to be the aim, the rule, and the end of all laws."[20]

This "Moral Law"—argues Calvin—proceeds "from the Source of rectitude Himself, and from the natural feelings implanted in us by Him." For "it flows from the Fountain of Nature . . . and is founded on the general principle of all laws."[21]

"Adam was at first created as the image of God, so that he might reflect as in a mirror the righteousness of God. . . . This is that Law of Nature which common sense declares to be inviolable. . . . You take righteousness, in general, as uprightness."[22]

On Genesis 2:15–17, Calvin says: "Man was the governor of the World. . . . A Law is imposed upon him, in token of his subjection. . . . Paul does not deny that God from the beginning imposed a Law upon man for the purpose of maintaining the right due to Himself." Calvin, incidentally, was a trained Jurist—and wrote the posthumously published *Juridical Lexicon of Both Imperial and Canon Law* (1670).

Calvin, in his *Institutes of the Christian Religion*, writes, "The prohibition to touch the tree of the knowledge of good and evil was a trial of obedience—so that, by passing the test, Adam might prove his willing submission to God's command. . . ."

He continues: "'Whenever the Heathen who do not have the Law, by nature do the things contained in the Law, these . . . show the work of the Law written in their hearts, their consciences also bearing witness and their thoughts meanwhile accusing or else excusing one another' (Romans 2:14–15). If the Heathen have the righteousness of the Law naturally engraved on their minds, we certainly cannot say that they are altogether blind as to the rule of life. Nothing indeed is more common than for man to be sufficiently instructed in a right course of conduct by the Law of Nature, of which the Apostle here speaks. . . . The end of the Law of Nature, therefore, is to render man inexcusable. . . . The Divine Law . . . is a perfect standard of righteousness. . . .

"The Ten Commandments of the Law . . . which God originally prescribed, is still in force. . . . The very things contained in the Two Tables are, in a manner, dictated to us by that internal Law which as has been already said is in a manner written and stamped on every heart. For conscience . . . points out the distinction between good and evil, and thereby convicts us of departure from duty." [23]

The Decalogue
from
Fall to Flood

$\mathscr{A}$LSO after the Fall and before the Flood, the Decalogue was universally known. The lives of all of Adam's descendants—both the regenerate and the unregenerate—provide clear evidence of consciousness of the Ten Commandments.

Noah, for example, is not only called a righteous man, but is also referred to as a law-abiding man (Genesis 6:9). But he also trusted God alone and longed for the promised Messiah (Genesis 4:1, 5:29: cf. the First Commandment). Enoch the Sethite and Noah both walked with God and pleased Him (Genesis 5:24, 6:9: cf. the Second Commandment). The Sethites as a group "began calling on the Name of the Lord"; and Lamech the Cainite swore an unholy oath (Genesis 4:23–26: cf. the Third Commandment).

And Abel and Noah apparently kept the Sabbath (Genesis 2:3, 4:3, 5:29, 7:4–10, 8:6–12, & 8:20–22: cf. the Fourth Commandment).[24]

The Sethites were apparently called "sons of God"; and Ham was punished for dishonoring his father (Luke 3:38; Genesis 6:4, 9:22–25: cf. the Fifth Commandment). Cain sinned by killing Abel (Genesis 4:11, 23; First John 3:10–15: cf. the Sixth Commandment), and "sin" is the transgression of the Law (First John 3:4).

Lamech the Cainite was the first bigamist, and the "sons of God" or the Sethite men immorally cohabited with the faithless "daughters of men" or the Cainite women (Genesis 4:19–23, 6:1–5: cf. the Seventh Commandment). Noah in the ark provided food to his family and to his animals (Genesis 6:21–22: cf. the Eighth Commandment). Cain lied to God (Genesis 4:9: cf. First John 3:10–15; & John 8:44: cf. the Ninth Commandment). And the believing sons of God sinfully desired the faithless daughters of men (Genesis 6:2: cf. the Tenth Commandment).

Luther rightly demanded that also "we must firmly establish civil law and the sword"—in order to punish murderers and other evil-doers. "The penal law existed from the beginning of the World. For when Cain slew his brother, he in turn was in . . . great terror of being killed. . . . He would not have had this fear, if he had not seen and heard from Adam that murderers should be slain. Moreover, God re-established and confirmed this after the Flood in unmistakable terms when He said: 'whosoever sheds man's blood, his blood shall be shed by man.'" (Genesis 9:1-6: cf. 1:26-28, 2:17).[25]

Calvin refers also to God's Sabbath rest: "Inasmuch as it was commended to men from the beginning that they might employ themselves in the worship of God—it is right that it should continue to the end of the World. . . . This institution has been given not to a single century or people, but to the entire human race. . . . It is not credible that the observance of the Sabbath was omitted when God revealed the rite of sacrifice to the holy Fathers (Genesis 4:2-4: cf. 7:4-10, 8:8-12, & 8:20-22), . . . God re-newed it (in Exodus 16 & 20)."[26]

God re-established—significantly, right after the Flood—His original Law-Covenant and its Dominion Charter with the family of Noah, who was a kind of second Adam (Genesis 9:1-9). The death penalty clearly implies the law against murder—the central Commandment in the Decalogue—in which God states: "Surely I will requite your blood of your lives. I will requite it at the hand of every animal, and at the hand of man. I will requite the life of man at the hand of every man's brother. Whosoever sheds a man's blood, his blood shall be shed by man. For God made man as His image" (Genesis 9:5-6).

This presupposes God's Law not only against murder, but also against adultery and blasphemy and theft and the breach of all the rest of the Ten Commandments. Thus the Hebrew *Talmud*, referring to these universal Noachic laws, admirably summarizes: "Seven precepts were imposed on the descendants of Noah—civil justice, the prohibition of blasphemy, idolatry, incest, murder, theft, and the prohibition of eating flesh cut from a living animal."[27]

These are examples of many of the Decalogue's own Ten Commandments. No wonder, then, that the Christian Council of Jerusalem ordained for converted Gentiles "that they should abstain from pollutions of idols, and from fornication, and from things strangled, and from blood" (Acts 15:19ff.). For such are "necessary things"—if one would "do well" (Acts 15:28ff.: cf. James 1:25, 2:8-13, 3:9ff., & 4:4:11ff.).

Calvin comments on Genesis 9:1-10 (see endnote [26]), regarding Noah and his family right after the Flood, "that God blessed Noah and his sons. He does not simply mean that the favour of fruitfulness was *restored* to them; but that, at the same time, the design of God concerning the new restitution of the World was revealed unto them. . . .

"Thus He not only re-news the World by the same Word by which He before created it. But He directs His Word to men, in order that they may re-cover the lawful use of marriage . . . and may have confidence that a progeny shall spring from them which shall diffuse itself through all regions of the Earth so as to render it again inhabited. . . .

"This also has respect chiefly to the restoration of the World. . . . Remains of that dominion . . . which God had conferred on him [man] in the beginning, were still left. He now also promises that the same dominion shall continue. . . . God here does not bestow on men more than He had previously given, but only re-stores. . . . The Celestial Creator Himself, however corrupted man may be, still keeps in view the end of His original creation. . . . God, [re-]making His Covenant with the sons of Noah, commands them to hope for the best. . . . It was not, therefore, a private Covenant confirmed with one family only, but one which is common to all people and which shall flourish in all ages to the end of the World. . . . God, as in a matter of present concern, makes a Covenant with Noah and his family. . . . Secondly, He transmits His Covenant to posterity."

John Selden was a very important antiquarian, barrister, theologian, and Member of the Westminster Assembly in seventeenth century England. Later, he was appointed Keeper of the Rolls. In his celebrated book, *On the Law of Nature and of the Gentiles*, Selden wrote that the Law of Nature derives via Noah from

Eden.[28] Selden also gave his learned views on the later influence of the Ancient Hebrews, the Ancient Egyptians, and the Ancient Phoenicians.[29] He further referred to Pythagoras on the one hand, and to the Common Law of Britain's Ancient Druids on the other (as also does Blackstone).

The Decalogue
in the Patriarchs and
the Prophets

*W*HEN God repromulgated the Covenant and gave its Dominion Charter (implying the Ten Commandments)[30] to Noah after the Flood (Genesis 9:1-7), more evidence appears of man's knowledge of the Ten Commandments. And this is before their official re-announcement through Moses to Israel on Mount Sinai.

Sadly, however, post-flood man soon sought a one world government at the tower in the City of Babel (Genesis 11:1-9). This was not one nation under God. Instead, it was many nations under the heel of the ungodly Nimrod—the tyrant or "mighty man" of violence.

Babel mirrored Cain's ungodly "Enoch City" before it (Genesis 4:16-24). For Babel became simply "the empire of fallen man" all over again (Genesis 6:1-5: cf. 10:8-12).

But God destroyed Nimrod's despotic and cosmopolitan tyranny (Genesis 11:1-9). For God had originally created mankind in order that it should leave its Edenic dwelling place—and start moving out into all the World, thus developing into the various distinct nations (Genesis 1:28, 2:7ff., 2:24ff., 3:24; Acts 17:26ff.).

Henceforth, until Christ came, the nations of mankind developed separately. Their boundaries would now be set according to the number of Abraham's descendants, the children of Israel or God's Ancient Covenant People (Deuteronomy 32:8).

Ancient Greek, Ancient Roman, and also Ancient Celtic law were all formed much later than the Mosaic Decalogue. Remarkably, however, they all show traces of the Pre-Mosaic Decalogue—as also do the Ancient Law Codes of India and China, etc.

Both before and after Abraham, sin promoted separation between the various nations and especially between God-fearing nations and God-ignoring nations. Mercifully, however, it is also true that God-fearing individuals in one nation often gladly fellowshipped with God fearers among other nations. But God-haters in all nations stand together against God-fearers, even in their own nation (Psalm 2:1ff.; Matthew 25:32ff.; Acts 17:26-34).

In 1976, the Tell Mardikh tablets were unearthed at Ebla in Syria. They apparently date from at least 2300

B.C. They preserve the ancient divine name *Jehovah* and the word *Elohim* as well as contain accounts of Adam's creation and of Noah's Flood.

They also allude to both Heber and his descendant Abraham, and mention Sodom and Gomorrah. They also describe in detail both mercantile treaties and international trade emanating from the Near East[31] (Genesis chaps. 1-8, 10:24-25, 11:14-27ff., 14:8-14ff., 18:22ff.).

According to Dr. David Noel Freedman, a University of Michigan Archaeologist, two tablets of this *Ebla Code* deal with case law and reveal that the later great law codes originated not with the Babylonian Emperor Hammurabi, but earlier—back in the time of Ebla—or perhaps even more anciently still.[32]

One of these two legal tablets deals with damages to be awarded to injured parties. A blow inflicted by a hand, without a weapon, was worth five lambs. An injury caused by a weapon, was redeemed by the payment of fifty cattle (cf. God's Sixth Commandment).

The other tablet concerns illicit sexual relations with unmarried women. That code provides that if a man had intercourse with a single woman who was not then a virgin, he had to pay a fine to her father or guardian. If the woman was a virgin, the man went on trial. And if the trial determined that the woman had been forced and raped—the man was adjudged

guilty and sentenced to death (cf. God's Seventh
Commandment; Genesis 4:8ff., 6:2–9ff., 12:17ff., 14:8–
24, 34:2–7ff.; Exodus chaps. 21–23; & Deuteronomy
22:25–29, etc.).

Even the more perverted and despotic Sumerian laws
reflected in the later Babylonian laws of Hammurabi—
like those of the Hamite Nimrod himself (Genesis
10:6–12: cf. 11:1–9), can, in the last analysis, ground
themselves only in Pre-Abrahamic Law. From this the
Sumerians progressively departed (Genesis 9:22–25,
10:6–12, 11:1–9, 12:1–8; & Joshua 24:2ff.).

The *Codex Hammurabi* was discovered in A.D. 1902
at Susa in ancient Elamitic Mesopotamia. Later, in
A.D. 1928, Dr. J. H. Hertz, before the Society for
Jewish Jurisprudence, presented a paper on "Ancient
Semitic Codes and the Mosaic Legislation." Dr. Hertz
delivered it in London's Inner Temple, the historic
shrine of British Common Law.

In 1938, Leiden's Professor Dr. Martin David,
the eminent authority on Ancient Babylonian and
Assyrian Law, put Hammurabi's reign at *circa* 1955–
1913 B.C.[33] Then, writing in A.D. 1959, Chicago's Law
Professor Dr. Palmer D. Edmunds, in his book *Law
and Civilization,* described Hammurabi as a king who
was a contemporary of Abraham.[34]

In light of the later discovery of the Tell Mardikh tablets, we now know that Abraham antedated Hammurabi.

Consequently, it can no longer credibly be maintained that the 'Abrahamic' [sic] Mosaic Law "evolved" from the *Codex Hammurabi*. Hammurabi's *Babylonian Code* is a degeneration not just of Pre-Abrahamic Proto-Semitic Law, but perhaps even of the Laws of the Chaldean Abraham himself or of his contemporaries (Genesis 9:26ff., 11:14–26, 14:1–13ff., 18:18–19, 26:5).

Significantly, even Chicago's Professor Dr. G. A. F. Knight in his 1962 book, *Law and Grace*—published before the discovery of the Tell Mardikh tablets—apparently dated Sumeria's renowned *Codex Hammurabi* more than a century after Abraham.[35] Further, it is now also known that the Law Codes of Ancient Greece and Rome, and the Common Law of the Celts, and the laws even of Ancient China and India were not just Post-Abrahamic but even Post-Mosaic.

The Pre-Mosaic Abraham commanded his children to "keep the way of the Lord [and] to do justice and judgment" (Genesis 18:19). According to God Himself, Abraham "kept My charge, My Commandments, My statutes, and My Laws" (Genesis 26:5). Would that all Christians, as "children of Abraham" (Galatians 3:29), may do the same!

God revealed Himself to Abraham as the one and only "God Almighty" (Genesis 17:1: cf. the First Commandment). He commanded Jacob's household to "put away your strange gods" or images (Genesis

43

31:19, 30, & 35:2-4: cf. the Second Commandment). God swore by Himself to Abraham; but Esau was a profane person (Genesis 22:16; & Hebrews 6:13ff., 12:16: cf. the Third Commandment). The week is only demarcated by means of an initial or a final holy day[36]—and Job, Jacob, Laban, Joseph, the Egyptians, the pre-Sinaitic Israelites, and possibly even Balaam of Mesopotamia all knew about the week (Genesis 29:27-28, 31:23, chpters 41-43, 50:10; Exodus 5: 4-5, 7:25, 16:4-30; & Numbers 22:5, 23:1, 19, & 29:32: cf. the Fourth Commandment).

Lot's daughters, Ishmael, Esau and Jacob all deceived or mocked their elders—which was clearly regarded as sinful (Genesis 19:30-38, 21:9, 25:9, 26:34-35, & 27:21-35: cf. the Fifth Commandment). Abraham was not to hurt Isaac, and Laban was warned by God not to harm Jacob (Genesis 22:12, 31:24-29: cf. the Sixth Commandment). Pharaoh, Lot's daughters, Abimelech and the Shechemites all recognized that adultery was sin, as did Jacob and Judah and Joseph (Genesis 12:11-18, 19:30-38, 20:2-18, 26:9-10, 34:1-7, 35:22, 38:13-24, 39:7-9, & 49:3-4: cf. the Seventh Commandment). Rachel's theft and Joseph's being kidnapped were both regarded as transgressions, and all of Joseph's brothers acknowledged that theft was wrong (Genesis 31:32, 37:28, 44:1-2, 45:3-5, & 50:15-20: cf. the Eighth Commandment). The lies of

Abraham and Isaac and Jacob and Joseph's brothers were all reprehensible (Genesis 12:11–13, 20:2–9, 26:7, 27:24, & 37:10: cf. the Ninth Commandment). And Lot's greed almost cost him his life (Genesis 13:10, 19:15–24: cf. the Tenth Commandment).

Moreover, all ten of God's Commandments were apparently well known to Job of old (on the basis of his involvement with God's Covenant with Adam). This is very significant, for Job lived and died outside the confines of the Ancient Israelites, God's Covenant People (Job 31, esp. vv. 1, 33, & 40: cf. chaps. 1–2, esp. 2:13).

God repromulgated the Ten Commandments to Moses on Mount Sinai in Exodus 20 and again some 40 years thereafter.[37] Note especially the word "remember" in Exodus 20:8 (cf. also 16:28ff.), as well as the Decalogue according to Deuteronomy 5:1–24. Even the Later Prophets all condemned breaches of each Commandment of the Decalogue (cf. Isaiah chaps. 56–59; Daniel chaps. 3–6; Hosea chap. 6; Amos chaps. 2–6; & Malachi chaps. 1–4).

The Decalogue in
the Person and Teaching
of Christ

THE relationship between the Ten Commandments and the Person of Jesus Christ our Lord
provides similar instruction. He, "the righteous" One
(First John 2:1), declared Himself to be God (John
8:58, 20:28: cf. the First Commandment). He is also
described as the unique and essential image of the
unseen God (Hebrews 1:1–3; Colossians 1:13–15: cf.
the Second Commandment). Apart from the Name of
Jesus, there is no other Name under Heaven whereby
we must be saved (Acts 4:12: cf. the Third Commandment). Moreover, He is the Lord of the Sabbath (Mark
2:28: cf. the Fourth Commandment).

He is also One with the Father (John 10:30: cf.
the Fifth Commandment). He is the Living One
(Revelation 1:18: cf. the Sixth Commandment). He is
the Faithful and True (Revelation 19:11: cf. the Seventh

Commandment). He is the Giver of the Comforter (John 14:16: cf. the Eighth Commandment). He is the Truth (John 14:6: cf. the Ninth Commandment). And He is the Desire of all nations (Haggai 2:7: cf. the Tenth Commandment).

Furthermore, Christ's teachings include a strong emphasis on keeping the whole Decalogue. For they are thoroughly consistent with the essential righteousness of His Own Law-abiding Person.

Jesus Himself taught: "Do not think that I have come to demolish the Law or the Prophets! I have not come to demolish, but to finish constructing. For truly I tell you, till Heaven and Earth pass away not one jot or tittle shall in any way pass from the Law till all be fulfilled. Thus, whosoever shall break one of these least Commandments and shall teach men so—shall be called the least as regards the Kingdom of Heaven." (Matthew 5:17-19).

Calvin here comments: "Christ therefore now declares that His doctrine is so far from being at variance with the Law, that it agrees perfectly with the Law and the Prophets. . . . Devout worshippers of God would never have embraced the Gospel, if it had been a revolt from the Law. . . . He immediately adds, by way of confirmation, that it is impossible for even one point of the Law to fail—and pronounces a curse on those teachers who do not faithfully labor to maintain its authority. . . . We must not imagine that the coming of Christ has freed us from the authority of the Law. For it is the eternal rule of a devout and holy life and must therefore be as unchangeable as the justice of God. . . .

"Christ here speaks expressly of the Commandments of Life or the Ten Words which all the children of God ought to take as the rule of their life. He therefore declares, that they are false and deceitful teachers who do not restrain their disciples within obedience to the Law, and that they who weaken the authority of the Law in the slightest degree—are unworthy to occupy a place in the Church. But the good and true Ministers of the Gospel are those who command the observance of the Law; both by the example of their lives and by their word."

Not only did Jesus teach that "the righteous shall be satisfied" (Matthew 5:6), but also that they should love the Lord their God (Matthew 22:37: cf. the First Commandment). He taught they should worship God in Spirit (John 4:24: cf. the Second Commandment). They should never blaspheme against the Holy Ghost (Matthew 12:31: cf. the Third Commandment). And they should keep the Sabbath (Luke 4:16, 23:56–24:1; Matthew 24:20: cf. the Fourth Commandment).

They should also honor their parents (Matthew 19:19: cf. the Fifth Commandment). They may not murder

(Matthew 19:18: cf. the Sixth Commandment). They are not to commit adultery (Matthew 5:27–28: cf. the Seventh Commandment). They are not to steal (Matthew 19:18: cf. the Eighth Commandment). They are not to swear at all (Matthew 5:34: cf. the Ninth Commandment). And they may not lustfully covet or desire (Matthew 5:28: cf. the Tenth Commandment).

Indeed, in His Great Commission, Christ demands that all of the Ten Commandments be taught to all baptized Christians and faithfully observed. "Go therefore and make all nations disciples, baptizing them [and] . . . teaching them to observe all things whatsoever I have commanded you."

This said He, the Word of God Who had commanded Adam to keep His Covenant's Laws. He it was Who had given the Ten Commandments to the Israelites on Mount Sinai; Who later warned His Christian disciples and, indeed, even the anti-christian Pharisees and all men everywhere not to break even the least of the Commandments of God (Matthew 5:19, 28:19; Mark 7:4; John 1:1–9, 1:14–18: cf. Exodus 20; & Genesis 1:1–28).

The Decalogue in History from Christ until Today

*A*FTER the close of the Bible's Book of Revelation, also the Didache (alias the circa A.D. 97 Teaching of the Twelve Apostles) declares: "There are two ways, one of life and one of death; but a great difference between the two ways. The way of life, then, is this: First, you shall love God Who made you! . . . And the second commandment of the Teaching: you shall not commit murder; you shall not commit adultery; you shall not commit paederasty [alias the sexual corruption of young children]; you shall not practise witchcraft; you shalt not murder a child by abortion, nor kill that which has been begotten! You shall not covet the things of your neighbor; you shall not forswear yourself; you shall not bear false witness!"[38] See Exodus 20:2–17.

Around A.D. 98, the Epistle of Barnabas clearly taught that God urges especially Christians: "You shall not forsake the Commandments of the Lord! . . . You shall not commit fornication; you shall not commit adultery; you shall not be a corrupter of youth [alias a sexual molester of children]! You shall not let the Word of God issue from your lips with any kind of impurity! . . . You shall not take the Name of the Lord in vain! . . . You shall not slay the child by procuring abortion; nor, again, shall you destroy it after it has been born! . . . You shall remember the Day of Judgment!"[39]

See again, Exodus 20:2–17!

It then concludes (about Genesis 2:2) that "the Sabbath is mentioned at the beginning of the creation: 'And God made in six days the works of His hands; and made an end on the seventh day, and rested on it, and sanctified it.'. . . Giving rest to all things, I shall make a beginning of the eighth day—that is, a beginning of another World. . . .

"Also, it is written concerning the Sabbath in the Decalogue which [the Lord] spoke face to face to Moses on Mount Sinai: 'And you must sanctify the Sabbath of the Lord with clean hands and a pure heart'. . . . Therefore also we [Christians] keep the eighth day with joyfulness—the day also on which Jesus rose again from the dead."[40]

Apparently around A.D. 99, the Apostle Paul's friend Clement, the Christian Overseer in Rome (cf. Philippians 4:3), wrote his First Epistle to the Corinthians. There, Clement assures the Church: "The Commandments and Ordinances of the Lord were written upon the tablets of your hearts." (cf. Proverbs 7:1-3).

Even before the end of the first century, Clement also indicated that both the Law and the Gospel had even reached what was probably even then known as the 'Western Isles'—viz. Britain and Ireland. For Clement also insisted that his friend the Apostle Paul had carried Christianity "to the end of the West."[41]

That Britain had received the Gospel long before that time, seems to be corroborated by the A.D. 116. Pagan Roman Historian Tacitus. He implies that the British noblewoman Pomponia had embraced Christianity in Britain around A.D. 41, at least two years before Pagan Rome's Emperor Claudius's invasion of Britain.[42] No wonder, then, that British Common Law, early fusing Decalogical Christianity with the considerable elements of the Ten Commandments in Ancient Celtic Druidism, has always stressed the Moral Law of God. See the 58ff. B.C. Julius Caesar's *Gallic Wars*.[43]

In A.D. 20, Polycarp of Smyrna enjoined both himself and other Christians to "do that which is good" and to "keep on walking in His Commandments and

. . . abstaining ourselves from all unrighteousness, covetousness, love of money, evil speaking, false witness [and] 'not rendering evil for evil or railing for railing.'"[44] (First Peter 3:9: cf. Exodus 20:2–17.) Similarly: Justin Martyr of Samaria,[45] Theophilus of Antioch,[46] and Athenagoras of Athens.[47]

In A.D. 180, Irenaeus of Lyons clearly taught: "The Lord [Jesus] did not abrogate the natural [precepts] of the Law. . . . In the beginning . . . God formed Adam [and Eve]. . . . God at the first indeed warned them by means of natural precepts which from the beginning He had implanted into mankind . . . by means of the Decalogue. . . . The Lord [Jesus] Himself did speak in His Own Person to all alike the words of the Decalogue. And therefore, in like manner, it remains permanently with us—receiving by means of His advent in the flesh extension and increase, but not abrogation."[48] Similarly, so also Clement of Alexandria in A.D. 190.[49]

In A.D. 200, Tertullian of Carthage says in his *Answer to the Jews* that God "in the beginning of the World . . . gave to Adam himself, and to Eve, a Law. . . . In this Law given to Adam, we recognize in embryo all the precepts which afterwards sprouted forth when given through Moses. That is—'you shall love the Lord your God from your whole heart and from your whole soul; you shall love your neighbor as yourself; you shall not kill; you shall not commit adultery; you shall not steal; false witness you shall not utter; honor your father and mother; and, that which is another's, you shall not covet.' For the Primordial Law was given to Adam and Eve in Paradise, as the womb of all the precepts of God. . . . Before the Law of Moses written on tablets of stone . . . there was an Unwritten Law which habitually was understood 'naturally' and which was habitually kept by the Fathers." [50]

Tertullian adds that "the Britons had been subjugated to Christ"—a statement verified by the later Early British Historians Gildas, Bede, and Nenni.[51] In A.D. 240, the Law-loving Origen of Caesarea adds that the "goodness" of the "Saviour is . . . among the Britons," too.[52] Even earlier, he explains, also "the Druids" were "most learned"—"on account of the resemblance between their traditions and those of the Jews." For even the Celts "worshipped the one God . . . previously to the coming of Christ" and "had long been predisposed to Christianity through the doctrines of the Druids . . . who had already inculcated the doctrine of the unity of the Godhead." The impact of God's Law and of Christianity also on British Common Law by the time of Origen is a matter of historical record.[53]

Within the next fifty years, persecuted Christianity grew greatly in the Roman Empire, and almost all of Britain became Christianized. According to Dr. Philip

Schaff, the great Church Historian, Constantine was born in Britain in 272 of a devout mother Helena, apparently the British Christian Princess Helen.[54] In 313, at York, he was crowned not just King of Britain but also the first Christian Emperor of the whole Roman Empire. He then turned against Paganism in public life, suppressed spellbinders and witchdoctors, urged all to keep the Lord's Day for Sabbath Rest, adopted the Law-loving Church Father Lactantius as his mentor, and started to enact Christian laws for Britain and his whole Empire.[55]

In 880, Alfred the Great, with help from the famous Welsh Scholar Asser, his mentor, codified the Ten Commandments and much of their case law and portions from the New Testament into English Common Law.[56] His successors—Athelstan, Canute, and Edward the Confessor—expanded this;[57] and William the Conqueror swore to uphold it.[58] *Magna Carta* enshrined it,[59] its Article 61 providing for last-resort rebellion against a king who follows his own corrupt political practices and who does not finally submit to the Law of God. So also did the 1689 British *Bill of Rights* (or the *Act for Declaring Rights and Liberties*).

Britain and her former Colonies such as Australia, Canada, and New Zealand inherited the Common Law with Christianity and the Ten Commandments as integral parts thereof. In 1788, the first Governor

(Sir Arthur Phillip) maintained the Decalogue throughout Australia's New South Wales.[60] Judge Hargrave stated in 1884 that the Law of God is part of the law of the Colony of New South Wales. He said: "All the revealed or Divine Law, so far as enacted by the Holy Scriptures to be of universal obligation, is part of our colonial law"; and "Christianity is part and parcel of our general laws."[61] And even the 1992 Supreme Court of Victoria stated that Australia is still "a predominantly Christian country."[62]

United States Law rests chiefly on Biblical Anglo-British Common Law. As University of Pennsylvania Law Professor Dr. F. S. Philbrick points out in an article on American Law, the Colonists brought the Common Law with them to America, as their very own birthright.[63] Along with English political traditions and precedents, that Common Law was transported across the Atlantic together with its concepts of property, liberty, and justice—with such of its rules as fitted colonial conditions. Half a dozen of the American Colonies endeavored to follow these laws from early on. In several Colonies, this position was accorded also to the Holy Scriptures themselves.

Blackstone was definitive for the law of both Australia and the United States from the first moment of their existence. In his *Analysis of the Laws of England,* he held: "Law is a rule of action prescribed by a superior power. . . . Natural Law is the rule of action, prescribed by the Creator, and discoverable by the light of reason. . . . The Divine or Revealed Law (considered as a rule of action) is also the Law of Nature, imparted by God Himself."[64] By this "Revealed Law" Blackstone meant: the Ten Commandments.

In his famous 1765 *Commentaries on the Laws of England*, Blackstone added:[65] "The Supreme Being formed the universe and created matter out of nothing. He impressed certain principles upon the matter from which it can never depart. . . . Laws in their more confined sense . . . denote the rules . . . of human action or conduct . . . by which man . . . is commanded to make use of these faculties. . . . Man, considered as a creature, must necessarily be subject to the laws of his Creator. For he is entirely a dependent being. Any human law must be in conformity with this basic Law of Nature, or it will not work. And, consequently, as man depends absolutely on his Maker for everything—it is necessary that he should in all points conform to his Maker's Will. . . . As He is also a Being of infinite wisdom, He has laid down only such laws as were founded in those relations of justice. . . .

"These are the eternal, immutable laws of good and evil to which the Creator in all His dispensations conforms; and which He has enabled human reason to discover. . . . This is the foundation of what we call ethics or Natural Law. . . . This Law of Nature, being coeval with mankind and dictated by God Himself, is of course superior in obligation to any other. It is binding over all the globe; in all countries; and at all times. No human laws are of any validity, if contrary to this. . . .

"If our reason were always (as in our first ancestor before his transgression) clear and perfect . . . we should need no other guide but this. But every man now finds the contrary in his own experience: that his reason is corrupt; and his understanding full of ignorance and error. This has given manifold occasion for the benign interposition of Divine Providence. . . . The doctrines . . . we call 'the revealed or Divine Law' . . . are to be found only in the Holy Scriptures. These precepts . . . are found . . . to be really a part of the original Law of Nature. . . . The Moral Precepts of this [Divine] Law are indeed of the same original with those of the Laws of Nature. . . .

"With regard to the antient Britons, from Caesar's [58ff. B.C.] account of the tenets and discipline of the antient Druids," in them "centred all the learning of these western parts." Students went then, Caesar tells us, "over to Britain . . . to be instructed" in "points which bear a great affinity and resemblance to some of the modern doctrines of our English Law. . . .

"The British as well as the Gallic druids committed all their laws . . . to memory. . . . Our antient lawyers, and particularly [the A.D. 1470 English Lord Chief Justice Sir John] Fortescue (c. 17), insist with abundance of warmth that these customs are as old as the Primitive Britons, and continued down through the several mutations of government and inhabitants to the present time unchanged and unadulterated. . . .

"An academic expounder of the laws . . . should be engaged . . . in tracing out the 'originals' and as it were the 'elements' of the law. . . . These originals should be traced to their fountains. . . , to the customs of the [Ancient] Britons and [Ancient] Germans, as recorded by Caesar [58ff. B.C.] and Tacitus [A.D. 98ff.]. . . .

"The antient collection of unwritten maxims and customs which is called the 'Common Law' . . . had subsisted immemorially in this kingdom [of Britain]. . . . It was then taught . . . in the monasteries, in the universities, and in the families of the principal nobility. The Clergy in particular as they then engrossed almost every other branch of learning so (like their predecessors the British Druids)[66] . . . were peculiarly remarkable for their proficiency in the study of the law. . . . The Judges therefore were usually created out of the sacred order."

In light of the above citations from Blackstone, Chicago Law Professor Edmunds observes that American Law is indebted to Natural Law concepts for much of its trend and content.[67] Thus one reads in the grand paragraph introducing the Declaration of Independence:

"When in the course of human events it becomes necessary for one people to dissolve the political bands which have connected them with another and to assume among the powers of the Earth the separate and equal station to which the Laws of nature and of nature's God entitle them—a decent respect to the opinions of mankind requires that they should declare the causes which impel them to the separation. We hold these truths to be self-evident: that all men are created equal; that they are endowed by their Creator with certain unalienable rights; that among these are life, liberty and the pursuit of happiness."

Further, the Seventh Amendment, an integral part of the original Constitution of the United States of America as first ratified, states that "in suits at Common Law . . . no fact tried by a jury shall be otherwise re-examined in any Court of the United States than according to the rules of the Common Law." Also, it is highly significant that after the conclusion of the Revolutionary War, the 1783 Peace Treaty of Paris between Great Britain and the United States was signed by both parties "in the Name of the Most Holy and Undivided Trinity."

When Queen Elizabeth II was crowned in 1953, she was given a Bible and enjoined: "This is the Royal

Law [cf. James 2:8–12]. . . . With this sword do justice; stop the growth of iniquity. . . ; help and defend widows and orphans; restore the things that are gone to decay; maintain the things that are restored; punish and reform what is amiss. . . . Remember that the whole World is subject to the power and Empire of Christ our Redeemer. . . . The Lord give you faithful Parliaments and quiet realms; sure defence against all enemies; fruitful lands and a prosperous industry; wise counsellors and upright magistrates; leaders of integrity in learning and labor; a devout, learned, and useful clergy; honest, peaceable and dutiful citizens!" (cf. Leviticus 26; & Deuteronomy 28).

In 1982, the Congress of the United States of America authorized and requested President Reagan to proclaim that "the Bible, the Word of God, has made a unique contribution in shaping the United States as a distinctive and blessed nation and people"; that "deeply held religious convictions springing from the Holy Scriptures led to the early settlement of our nation"; and that "Biblical teachings inspired concepts of civil government that are contained in our Declaration of Independence and the Constitution of the United States." Concluding that "the Bible is 'the rock on which our Republic rests,'" Congress further recognized "our national need to study and apply the teachings of the Holy Scriptures."

No wonder, then, that on May 21, 1988, British Prime Minister Margaret Thatcher also told the General Assembly of the Church of Scotland: "From the beginning, man has been endowed by God with the fundamental right to choose between good and evil. . . . We were made in God's Own image, and therefore we are expected to use all our own power of thought and judgment in exercising that choice. . . . If you try to take the fruits of Christianity without its roots, the fruits will wither. And they will not come [back] again, unless you nurture the roots. . . .

"The Old Testament lays down in Exodus the Ten Commandments. . . . By taking together these key elements . . . we gain: a view of the Universe; a proper attitude to work; and principles to shape economic and social life. We are told we must work and use our talents to create wealth. 'If a man will not work, he shall not eat'—wrote St. Paul to the Thessalonians [Second Epistle 3:10]. . . . You recall that Timothy was warned by St. Paul that anyone who neglects to provide for his own house . . . has disowned the faith and is 'worse than an infidel' [First Timothy 5:8]. . . .

"The Christian religion . . . is a fundamental part of our national heritage. For centuries, it has been our very lifeblood. Indeed, we are a nation whose ideals are founded on the Bible. . . . Also, it is quite impossible to understand our history or literature without grasping this fact. No majority can take away God-given human rights!"

What then is one to think today of killing human embryos and using them as ingredients for cosmetics? How should one regard attempts to clone human beings, and then to use their spare parts as medical panaceas for the uncloned? And what should one think of the present U.S. Supreme Court that strikes down anti-sodomy laws in Texas, but refuses to redress the removal of God's Ten Commandments from the Rotunda of the Supreme Court of Alabama?

True Christians
Love to
Keep God's Law

*L*UTHER insisted that "the Ten Commandments spread over the whole World not only before Moses, but even before Abraham and all the Patriarchs. For even if a Moses had never appeared and Abraham had never been born, the Ten Commandments would have had to rule in all men from the very beginning— as they indeed did, and still do. . . . We and all human beings are obligated to hear His Word, to honor father and mother, to refrain from murdering, from adultery, from stealing, from bearing false witness, from coveting. . . . All the Heathen bear witness to this in their writings. . . .

"God Himself . . . gives the universal Ten Commandments which . . . had been implanted at creation in the hearts of all men. . . . We and all Gentiles are just as duty-bound as the Jews to keep the First

Commandment, so that we have no other gods than the only God. . . .

"His Ten Commandments . . . pertain to all of mankind. . . . Each country and each household is duty-bound to observe the ordinances. . . . These are the Commandments of God Who ordained all the governments of the World."[68]

Deep in their hearts, all men know they should keep the Ten Commandments. In Romans 2:14ff., the Apostle Paul says that even "whenever Heathen who do not have the Law, by nature do the things contained in the Law," they "show the work of the Law written in their hearts, their conscience also bearing witness and their thoughts meanwhile accusing or else excusing one another in the Day when God shall judge the secrets of men by Jesus Christ."

On this, Calvin comments "that all the Gentiles alike . . . make laws to punish adultery, theft, and murder; and commend good faith in commercial transactions and contracts. In this way, they prove their knowledge . . . that adultery, theft, and murder are evils; and that honesty is to be esteemed. . . . There is, therefore, a certain natural knowledge of the Law—which states that one action is good and worthy of being followed, while another is to be shunned with horror."

Consequently, especially New Testament Christians will obey Christ's teachings about the need of keeping the Ten Commandments today and throughout the future too. The New Testament teaches that Christians have been saved and made righteous by Christ's Own Law-keeping. By grace and through faith in Christ's Own substitutionary Law-keeping alone, the merits of His obedience to the Law are imputed to His children as if they themselves had kept it impeccably.

When God the Father's children are regenerated, He gives them His Own Holy Spirit, the Spirit of God the Son. That Spirit then indwells them and, while writing His Laws on their hearts, by His sanctifying grace gives them an ever greater desire to keep the Ten Commandments to the glory of God. And they do this as a token of their gratitude for so great a salvation graciously donated to them on the basis of the matchless merits of the death of their Law-abiding Savior (Romans 3:36, 6:1-2, 7:6-25, 8:1-4; Second Corinthians 3:3-18; Hebrews 8:10).

Out of gratitude for so great a salvation, then, true Christians more and more worship "only one God" (First Corinthians 8:4-6: cf. the First Commandment). They "flee from idolatry" (First Corinthians 10:14: cf. the Second Commandment). "Above all," they "do not swear" (James 5:12: cf. the Third Commandment). And they acknowledge "there remains a [weekly] Sabbath-keeping for the people of God." (Hebrews 10:25, 4:9: cf. the Fourth Commandment).[69]

They "honor their fathers and mothers" (Ephesians 6:3: cf. the Fifth Commandment). They do not hate their brethren, as murderers do (First John 3:15: cf. the Sixth Commandment). They are not enemies of God, as adulterers are (James 4:4; Hebrews 13:4: cf. the Seventh Commandment). They "steal no more." (Ephesians 4:28: cf. the Eighth Commandment). They "do not lie to one another" (Colossians 3:9: cf. the Ninth Commandment). And they do not even name the sin of covetousness (Ephesians 5:5-12; First John 2:16: cf. the Tenth Commandment).

This means, as explained by the *Westminster Larger Catechism* 92-151, that they love God and (among many other sins) condemn atheism, polytheism, heresy, distrust, despair, presumptuousness, indiscreet zeal, lukewarmness, apostasy, angel-worship and fortune-telling—in terms of the First Commandment. They eagerly receive the Bible and the Sacraments and condemn idolatry and superstitions—in terms of the Second Commandment.

They love God's Name, and condemn irreverence and profanity and blasphemy and talismans and hypocrisy and backsliding—in terms of the Third Commandment. And they love their work on weekdays and God's Sabbath on weekends, and condemn its being desecrated by idleness and needless works and recreations—in terms of the Fourth Commandment.

They love their parents and children and employers and employees and preachers and parishioners and governments and citizens, and condemn disrespect of any of them—in terms of the Fifth Commandment. They love human life and health, and condemn unlawful attacks on either—in terms of the Sixth Commandment. They love chastity and their spouses, and condemn adultery and fornication and rape and incest and sodomy and impure gestures and scanty clothing and brothels and enforced celibacy and pornography—in terms of the Seventh Commandment.

They love faithfulness in contracts and their property and frugality, and condemn theft and robbery and kidnapping and extortion and bribery and vexatious lawsuits and gambling—in terms of the Eighth Commandment. They love truthfulness and sincerity and justice, and condemn lies and perjury and slander and libel and forgery and gossip and flattery and bragging and rumor-mongering—in terms of the Ninth Commandment. And they love contentedness, and condemn envy—in terms of the Tenth Commandment.

Law-keepers in Heaven
and
Law-breakers in Hell

*C*HRISTIANS know they will still be keeping God's Law on the New Earth to come, and thenceforth forevermore. They shall inherit God's Kingdom and righteousness (Matthew 6:33) and shall serve the Lord God Almighty (Revelation 21:22, 22:9: cf. the First Commandment). They know that idolaters shall be outside the New Jerusalem (Revelation 22:15: cf. the Second Commandment), and that sorcerers shall be thrown into the lake of fire (Revelation 22:15: cf. the Third Commandment). For Christians shall enter into God's rest and His everlasting Sabbath—while the wicked shall have no rest, day or night (Psalm 95:11; Isaiah 57:20–21, 66:23–24; Hebrews 4:11; Revelation 14:11-13: cf. the Fourth Commandment).

Christian peacemakers have a great reward with their heavenly Father (Matthew 5:9–12), whereas unbelievers shall be with their father the devil in Hell forever (John 8:44: cf. the Fifth Commandment). Commandment-keepers shall have right to the tree of life, while all murderers shall be outside in the pool of burning brimstone (Revelation 22:14–15: cf. the Sixth Commandment). Indeed, no whoremongers but only the pure in heart shall see God (Matthew 5:8; First Corinthians 6:9; Revelation 21:8: cf. the Seventh Commandment).

Only the generous but no thieves shall inherit God's Kingdom (First Corinthians 6:10: cf. the Eighth Commandment). Only the truthful shall be in the City of God; for outside are whosoever loves and tells lies (Revelation 22:15: cf. the Ninth Commandment). For the greedy shall be lost, while only those who hunger after righteousness shall be satisfied (Matthew 5:6; First Corinthians 6:10: cf. the Tenth Commandment).

Those who by Christ's grace keep the Covenant and execute the Dominion Charter and its Ten Commandments shall reign with Him as kings forever (Genesis 1:28, 17:6–7; Psalm 8; Revelation 21:24–26, 22:5). However, all Covenant-breakers and despisers of God's Moral Law—shall be cut off from God's people unto all eternity (Genesis 2:17: cf. 17:14; & Revelation 14:9–11, 19:20, 20:12–15, 21:8, 22:15).

This is what the Lord says: "To the Law and to the testimony! If they do not speak according to this

Word, it is because there is no light in them" (Isaiah 8:20).

So then: "If you wish to enter into life, keep the Commandments!"—said Jesus Christ the Lord to the rich young ruler (Matthew 19:17). Moreover, the inspired Apostle Paul, writing infallibly to saved Christians, after referring specifically to the Tenth Commandment, insists that "the Law is holy; and the Commandment holy and just and good and spiritual" (Romans 7:6, 9, 11, 14).

Elsewhere, Paul firmly emphasizes that all Christians are meticulously to observe the Fifth Commandment (Ephesians 6:1-3). Furthermore, the inspired Apostle James infallibly insists that saved Christians are to keep all Ten Commandments (James 1:1-2, 25, 2:1, 8-15, 3:9, 4:11-12).

Indeed, the equally-inspired Apostle John stresses that God's children must try to keep His Commandments (First John 3:2-3: cf. 3:4, 15, 24). "Here is the patience of the saints: here are they that keep the Commandments of God AND the faith of Jesus" also known as the Christian Faith (Revelation 14:12).

"Blessed is the man that does not walk in the counsel of the ungodly, nor stand on the way of sinners, nor sit in the seat of the scornful. But his delight is in the Law of the Lord: and in His Law he meditates day and night" (Psalm 1:1-2: cf. Psalms 19, & 119).

Blessed indeed is he who can say with the converted Paul: "I delight in the Law of God according to the inward man. . . . I thank God through Jesus Christ our Lord! So then, with the mind, I myself serve the Law of God!" (Romans 7:22-25: cf. 13:8-10; & First Corinthians 9:21b).

Dear reader! Are you really saved? Do you delight in the Law of God, and eagerly keep His Commandments? O, listen to the voice of Jesus! Hear the Word of Christ the Lord: "Why do you keep on calling Me 'Lord'—but not doing the things I say?" (Luke 6:46).

"If you love Me, keep My Commandments!"—says Jesus (John 14:15). Do you love Him?

Endnotes

1 F. Rabelais: *The Abbey of Theleme*, quoted in *White's Utopias of the Renaissance* (New York: Farrar Straus, 1955), 127ff.

2 F. N. Lee: *Communist Eschatology* (Nutley, N. J., U.S.A.: The Craig Press, 1974), 75–76. Cf. Cohn's *The Pursuit of the Millennium* (London: Mercury Books, 1962), 293–94.

3 I offer such an analysis in F. N. Lee: *The Covenantal Sabbath* (London: Lord's Day Observance Society, 1971), 343.

4 See *Heidelberg Catechism* Q. & A. 12 ("Since then by the righteous judgment of God we deserve temporal and eternal punishment, what is required so that we may escape this punishment and again be received into favor?"); *Belgic Confession* XIV & XVII; Kuyper's *E Voto Dordraceno* (Amsterdam, Netherlands: Wormser, 1892), I:81; & esp. Ridderbos's *De Theologische Cultuurbeschouwing van Abraham Kuyper* (Kampen, Netherlands: J. H. Kok, 1947), 289.

5 See H. Dooyeweerd: *A New Critique of Theoretical Thought* (Philadelphia, U.S.A.: Presbyterian & Reformed Pub. Co., 1953), I, 93, 99ff.

6 I Cor. 14:26, 33, 34, 37, 40. Cf. also Frame and Coppes: *The Amsterdam Philosophy* (Phillipsburg, N.J., U.S.A.: Harmony Press, n.d.), 27–31.

7 Lee: *Cov. Sab.*, 23–25.

8 A. Kuyper: *De Leer der Verbonden* (Kampen, Netherlands: J. H. Kok, 1909), 89. Cf. Lee's *Cov. Sab.*, 231, 47; W. Geesink's *Gereformeerde Ethiek* (Kampen, Netherlands: J. H. Kok, 1931), I, 35; G. B. Wurth's *Het Christelijk Leven* (Kampen, Netherlands: J. H. Kok, 1957), I:107; L. Berkhof's *Systematic Theology* (London: The Banner of Truth Trust, 1959), 216ff.; and H. Bavinck's *Gereformeerde Dogmatiek* (Kampen, Netherlands: J. H. Kok, 1928), II:533–36.

9 Lee: *Calvin on the Sciences* (London: Sovereign Grace Union, 1969), 16–19. Cf. Acts 14:17, 17:22–28; Rom. 1:20, 2:14–16; John 1:1–9; Gen. 4:20–22, 6:1–4, esp. v. 3: cf. Job 32:8, & Prov. 20:27: cf. Gen. 5:1–3, 9:1–6 & Jas. 3:9.

10 A. A. Hodge: *Outlines of Theology* (Edinburgh: Nelson, 1879), ch. XVII. cf. also Kuyper: *De Leer der Verbonden*. cf. Lee: *The Cov. Sab.*, 17–40, which quotes also Bavinck, Aalders, etc., with approval.

11 The great Polish Reformer John á Lasco, who supervised the Foreign Protestant Congregation in London under King Edward VI, had great influence in West Germany and the Netherlands and Poland and England. He believed that the Sabbath Commandment enjoined • both labor on the weekdays and rest on the Lord's Day. For "Laski • also emphasised the external Sabbath whereby the believer 'must work zealously for six days a week in a God-honoring occupation'; 'must encourage his family' to attend divine worship on the Sunday Sabbath 'according to the Commandment instituted and ordained by Christ'; 'must spend the whole day in service of one's neighbor and other holy works'; and must not 'break or desecrate the Sabbath Day destined for service of the Church in servile works—in idleness, jest, drunkenness, gambling, play and other works of the flesh'" (Lee's *Cov. Sab.*, 254–55).

12 It is of very great importance indeed to realize that it was probably the influence of Laski on Abraham Kuyper, Sr. (who wrote his doctoral dissertation on that Polish Reformer), which helped produce both Kuyper's "Sabbath Doctrine" (in his *Tractaat van den Sabbath* and his *Gomer voor den Sabbath* and his *E Voto Dordraceno*) on the one hand and his great cultural insights into Gen. 1:28, etc. (in his *Gemeene Gratie* and his *Pro Rege* and his *Stone Lectures*) on the other hand. The "Dominion Charter" and the weekly "Sabbath Day," thus stand or fall together. See also n. 13 below.

13 cf. also Martin Luther: "On the morning after the creation of Adam and Eve, that is, on the morning of the Sabbath Day, Adam and Eve were mindful of the will of God, etc. Thus Adam and Eve, flowering in innocence and original righteousness, and full of security on account of their trust in the most kind God, walked around naked, holding fast to the word and mandate of God, and praising God, as befits the Sabbath Day." Elsewhere Luther has claimed: "If Adam had stood in his innocency, yet he should have kept the seventh day holy. i.e., on that day he should have taught his children what was the will of God; and wherein His worship did consist; he should have praised God, given thanks, and offered"—that is, performed

an act of (unbloody) sacrifice—F. N. Lee. "On the other days he would have tilled his ground, looked to his cattle." For "Adam was to gather with his descendants on the Sabbath at the tree of life," i.e., at a small orchard of trees of the same species. "And when they had together eaten of the tree of life, to preach, i.e., to proclaim God, and His praises, and the glory of creation, . . . and to exhort them to a holy and sinless life and to a faithful tilling and keeping of the garden."

14 M'Crie (ed.): *The Marrow of Modern Divinity*.

15 Lee's *Cov. Sab.*, 46, n. 134.

16 Ibid., 23-25, 81-83.

17 M. Luther: *Second Dispute against the Antinomians*, 12th Jan. 1538, in *Werke*, Weimer ed., 39:I:478, 454.

18 Luther's translation of Hos. 6:7ff.: "Aber sie übertreten den Bund, wie Adam. . . . Denn Gilead is eine Stadt voll Abgötterei. . . . Wie die Ströter, so da lauern auf die Leute und würgen af dem Wege. . . . Den da huret Ephraim."

19 M. Luther: *Werke*, Weimer ed., 49:1ff.

20 J. Calvin: *Institutes of the Christian Religion*, IV:20:16.

21 J. Calvin: "Commentary on Leviticus 18:6," in *Harmony of the Pentateuch*, Eerdmans, Grand Rapids, 1968ff. III:100.

22 J. Calvin: "Commentary on Genesis 1:26-28" and "Commentary of Ephesians 4:24."

23 J. Calvin: *Institutes* (II:1:3ff., 2:22-24, 8:1).

24 F. N. Lee: *The Covenantal Sabbath*, ch. III.

25 M. Luther: *Secular Authority—To What Extent it Should be Obeyed*. In *Works*, Holman ed., Philadelphia, 1930, III:231ff.

26 J. Calvin: "Comm. on Gen. 2:1-3," "Comm. on Gen. 9:1-10," and "Comm. on Ex. 20" in *Harm. Pent.* II:437.

27 Sanhedrin 56a.

28 J. Selden: *De Jure Natura et Gentium*, in his *Omnia Opera*, I, 150–
51 (as per G. W. Johnson's summary in his *Memoirs of John Selden*,
London, 1835, 264ff.).

29 J. Selden: *Omnia Opera*, London, ed. D. Wilkins, 1726, I, 83, 89ff.

30 cf. our text above at notes 11 to 13.

31 See C. McIntire's *The Tell Mardikh Tablets*, 1976, 116 & esp. 8; and
H. J. Carlson's *Biblical and Archaeological Research*, in *Reports and
Messages of the Tenth World Congress of the International Council of
Christian Churches*, 1979, 84ff.—both published by the Christian
Beacon Press, Collingswood, N.J.

32 Ibid.

33 M. David: "Hammurabi" (art. in A. M. Hyamson & A. M. Silbermann:
Jewish Encyclopaedia, Shapiro Vallentine, London, 1938, IX & 265).

34 P. D. Edmunds: *Law and Civilization*, Public Affairs Press, Washington, D.C., 1959, 30.

35 Ibid., 20.

36 Lee's *Cov. Sab.*, 59–61, 70–72.

37 cf. "re-member" in Ex. 20:8, which suggests that the Sabbath (and,
by implication, the rest of the Decalogue also) had previously been
made known before Ex. 20.

38 *Did.* 1:1–2 & 2:1–2.

39 Epistle of Barnabas, 4, 12, 15, 19.

40 Ibid., 15.

41 Clement of Rome: *First Epistle to the Corinthians*, chs. 1, 2, 5.

42 Tacitus: *Annals* 31:32.

43 The Druids may well have been influenced by Hebrew crews on
Phoenician ships visiting the British Isles almost from the time of
Moses. Certainly ancient druidic religion reveals much trinitarian
influence; abhorred idolatry; upheld the death penalty for capital
crimes; and protected life, liberty, private property, and the pursuit
of happiness. See Addendum 8 ("Stonehenge and the Ancient-

British Druids") in F. N. Lee's *Common Law Roots and Fruits*, Samuel Rutherford School of Law, 1997, 2348-364—and cf. also in ch. 9 at 556-67. See Julius Caesar's (B.C. 58ff.) *Gallic Wars*, 4:20 to 6:24. cf. also Sir W. Blackstone's *Commentaries on the Laws of England*, Chicago University Press, 1979 rep., I:17-95—and our own endnotes 52 & 66 below.

44 Polycarp: *Epistle to the Philippians*, chs. 2 & 11.

45 Justin Martyr: *Second Apology*, chs. 2 & 4 & 15.

46 Theophilus: *To Autolycus*, 3:9.

47 Athenagoras: *A Plea for the Christians*, chs. 1-3 & 32-35.

48 Irenaeus: *Against Heresies*, IV:13:1 & 14:1-2 & 15:1 & 16:3-4.

49 Clement of Alexandria: *Exhortation to the Heathen*, ch. 4; his *Paedogogue* I:9 & III:11-12; and his *Miscellanies* II:2, 15, 18 & IV:3 & VII:16.

50 Tertullian: *Answer to the Jews*, chs. 2 & 4.

51 Ibid., ch. 9. See also Gildas's A.D. 570 *The Destruction of Britain* 5:1 to 8:1ff.; Bede's A.D. 731 *Ecclesiastical History of the English Nation* I:2-14; and Nenni(us)'s A.D. 796 *History of the Britons*, 19-31.

52 Origen: *Principles* II:4:1-2; *Homily 101 on Luke*; *Against Celsus* I:16; and his *Textual Criticism of Ezekiel*. See also our endnote 43 above.

53 See F. N. Lee: *Common Law Roots and Fruits*, 253ff. & 743-889.

54 P. Schaff: *History of the Christian Church*, Eerdmans, Grand Rapids, 1968 ed., III:18ff. & n. 2.

55 See Eusebius's *Church History* (I:1:1 to 2:1 & 9:6-9); his *Life of Constantine* I:8, 8, 25, 28-32 & II:20 & 23-24 & 27-28 & 42; IV:4-18 & 29 & 50-51 & 74-75; and his *Oration in Praise of the Emperor Constantine Pronounced on the Thirtieth Anniversary of his Reign* (Prologue & 1-3 & V:5-6 & VI:1 & IX:8-12 & XVI:2-12 & XVII:1-3 & XVII:11-14 & XVIII).

56 See F. N. Lee: *King Alfred the Great and Our Common Law*, at http://www.dr-fnlee.org/.

57 F. N. Lee: *Common Law* ch. 23, "English Common Law from Edward the Elder to Edward the Successor."

58 F. N. Lee: *Common Law*, ch. 24, "Anglo-Norman Common Law from Domesday Book to Magna Carta."

59 *Magna Carta: Preamble and Arts.* 1 & 20–55 and esp. 39: "We have also granted to all Freemen of our realm for us and our heirs for ever, all the liberties . . . to have and to hold for them and their heirs. . . . No Freeman shall be taken or imprisoned or dispossessed or outlawed . . . except by the legal judgment of his peers . . . or the law of the land. . . . A Freeman shall not be amerced [or fined] for a small offence. . . . We will sell to no man . . . either justice or right [by offering bribes]. . . . If any man has been dispossessed or deprived . . . without the lawful judgment of his peers—of his lands . . . or rights—we will forthwith restore them to him."

60 C. M. H. Clark: *A History of Australia*, 1973, I:78ff. & I:257ff.

61 *Ex parte Thackeray*, 13 S.C.R. (N.S.W.) 1, 61.

62 *Noontil v. Auty* (1992) 1 V.R. 365.

63 F. S. Philbrick: "American Law," in the *Encyclopaedia Britannica*, New York, 1929, I:777ff.

64 Sir W. Blackstone: *Tracts*, Clarendon, Oxford ed., 1771, 14.

65 Sir W. Blackstone: *Commentaries on the Laws of England*, Chicago University Press, 1979 rep., I:17, 35ff., 63ff., 73, 95, 39–40.

66 Op. cit., IV:401 & I:63ff. & 73 & 35 & 17. To support his own parenthetical statement that also the Ancient British Druids were *theological* Jurists "remarkable for their proficiency in the study of the Law," Blackstone here cites Caesar's (B.C. 58ff.) *De Bello Gallico* 6:12. See also our own endnote 43 above.

67 Op. cit., 187ff.

68 M. Luther: *Against the Sabbatarians*, in his *Werke*, Weimer ed., 39: I:356.

69 Lee's *Cov. Sab.*, 233–236.

Appendix

God's Eternal Moral Law (Part 1)

	Righteous-ness	Commandments				
		1st	2nd	3rd	4th	5th
God	John 1:25	John 17:3	John 4:24	Heb. 6:13	Gen. 2:2–3 cf. Heb. 4:3–4	Matt. 6:9
1st Adam	John 17:3	Gen. 3:11	Gen. 3:8 cf. 2 Cor. 11:3–4	Gen. 2:17	Gen. 2:2–3 cf. Psa. 95:11	Gen. 2:15–16 Gen. 3:11 Luke 3:38 Acts 17:28–29
Antediluvian Fathers	John 4:24	Gen. 4:1 Gen. 5:29	Gen. 5:24 Gen. 6:9	Gen. 4:23, 26	7 days in flood account at Gen. 4:3, 4; 5:29; 7:4, 10; 8:6–12	Gen. 6:2, 4 Luke 3:38 Gen. 9:22–25 (Ham's sin)
Postdiluvian Fathers	Heb. 4:3-4	Gen. 17:1	Gen. 31:19 Gen. 35:2–4	Gen. 22:16 Heb. 12:16	Jacob's Marriage Week Gen. 29:27, 28 (Job 2:13?)	Gen. 19:30–38 Gen. 21:9, 25:9 Gen. 27:21–24, 35 (Jacob's deception)
Moses	Gen. 2:2–3 cf. Heb. 4:3–4	Ex. 20:3	Ex. 20:4–6	Ex. 20:7	Ex. 20:8–11	Ex. 20:12
Teachings of Christ	Matt. 6:9	Matt. 22:37	John 4:24	Matt. 12:31	Luke 4:16	Matt. 19:19
2nd Adam (Christ)	Acts 14:15	John 8:58; 20:28	Rev. 5:12–14	Acts 4:12	Mark 2:28	John 10:30 John 4:34
NT Church (Present)	1 John 3:3	1 Cor. 8:4–6	1 Cor. 10:14	James 5:12	Heb. 4:9	Eph. 6:1–3
"New Jerusalem" (Eternal)	James 1:17 Psa. 50:9–10	Rev. 21:22; Rev. 22:9	Rev. 22:15 (Idolaters)	Rev. 22:15 (Sorcerers)	Psa. 95:11 Isa. 66:23 Heb. 4:11	Matt. 5:9, 12 (Peacemakers)
Unbelievers	Unbelievers	2 Cor. 4:4	Rev. 21:8 1 Pet. 4:4–5	Rev. 21:8 (Sorcerers)	Rev. 14:11	John 8:44

Francis Nigel Lee

God's Eternal Moral Law (Part 2)

Commandments					All Ten
6th	7th	8th	9th	10th	
Acts 14:15	1 John 3:3	James 1:17 Psa. 50:9–10	Heb. 6:18 Tit. 1:2	Ex. 20:5	Psa. 105:8
Gen. 2:7, 17	Gen. 2:18 Gen. 2:24	"stole" forbidden fruit, Gen. 2:17 cf. Gen. 3:7–11	Gen. 3:8, 10, 12	Gen. 3:6	Hos. 6:7
Gen. 4:11, 23	Gen. 4:19, 23 Gen. 6:1–5	Gen. 6:21–22 Noah gave what belonged to him	Gen. 4:9	Gen. 6:2	Gen. 6:18
Gen. 22:12 Gen. 30:24, 29	Gen. 19:30–38 (Lot & Daughters' Incest)	Gen. 31:32 Gen. 37:28 (Manstealing)	Gen. 12:11, 13	Gen. 13:10–11	Gal. 3:16–17
Ex. 20:13	Ex. 20:14	Ex. 20:15	Ex. 20:16	Ex. 20:17	Deut. 5:1–22
Matt. 19:18	Matt. 5:18	Matt. 19:18	Matt. 5:34, 37	Mark 7:22	Matt. 26:38
Rev. 1:18	Rev. 19:11 (Faithfulness to Bride)	John 14:16 John 10:18	John 14:6	Haggai 2:7 Matt. 8:20	Isa. 42:6
1 John 3:15	Jas. 4:4 Heb. 13:4	Eph. 4:28	Col. 3:10 Eph. 4:25	Eph. 5:5 Col. 3:5	Gal. 4:24–28
Rev. 22:15 (Murderers)	Matt. 5:8 1 Cor. 6:9 (Adulterers)	1 Cor. 6:10 (Thieves)	Rev. 22:15 (Makes a lie)	Matt. 5:6	Rev. 21:3 Tabernacle is God's Covenant Presence
Rev. 21:8 (Murderers)	Rev. 21:8 (Whoremongers)	1 Cor. 6:10 (Thieves)	Rev. 21:8 (All liars)	1 Cor. 6:10	Rom. 1:31 (Covenant breakers)

Theological Works by
Rev. Prof. Dr. Francis Nigel Lee
(Published 1957–2007)

The items below include all books, novels, poems, and other writings completed after he became a Christian in 1955. Page count is indicated at the end of items exceeding five pages. Dr. Lee has over 500 manuscripts completed but unpublished which are not listed here. Many of his writings are downloadable at: www.dr-fnlee.org

Mijn Bekering: Jezus Boeide Mij. Netherlands, Kortenhoef, 1960. 8 pp.

Grammar Book Becomes Living Word of God! South Africa, BFBS. 5 pp.

The Conversion of an Atheist. South Africa, NGK Pubs., 1961. 7 pp.

Die Woord as Woord van Oordeel. South Africa, *Polumnia*, 1962.

The Christian and the Law. South Africa, *Ichthus*, 1963.

Getuienis van 'n Voormalige Ateïs. South Africa, *Ons Jeug*, 1966.

The Sabbath in the Bible. England, Lord's Day Observance Soc., 1966. 20 pp.

Culture: Origin, Development, Goal. U.S.A.: Shelton Press, 1967. 27 pp.

Nationality and the Bible. U.S.A.: Shelton Press, 1967. 21 pp.

Communism vs. Christianity. U.S.A., LCICC, 1967. 20 pp.

The Biblical Theory of Christian Education. U.S.A.: Shelton Press, 1968. 20 pp.

Communism vs. Creation. U.S.A., Presbyterian & Reformed Pub. Co., 1969. 264 pp.

Calvin on the Sciences. England, Sovereign Grace Union, 1969. 48 pp.

Ras en Nasie. South Africa, Wever, 1969. 35 pp.

Materialisme; Idealisme; Calvinisme. South Africa, BSAVBCW, 1970. 8 pp.

Christian Philosophy in 20th Century North America. South Africa, BSAVBCW, 1970. 27 pp.

Die Dag van die Here. South Africa, NGK Commission for Public Morals, 1970. 20 pp.

A Christian Introduction to the History of Philosophy. U.S.A., Presb. & Ref. Pub. Co., 1970. 261 pp.

Die Grondgedagtes van die Kommunisme. South Africa, Antikom, 1971. 26 pp.

The Virgin Shall Conceive and Bear a Son. South Africa, Antikom, 1971.

The Salvation of Early-Dying Infants. South Africa, N.G.T.T., 1971. 15 pp.

Missions: The Heart of the Church's Calling. South Africa, *Nederduitse Gereformeerd Teologiese Tydskrif*, 1971. 17 pp.

The Covenantal Sabbath. London, England, Lord's Day Observance Society, 1971. 343 pp.

Julle Doop Mos Verkeerd! South Africa, NGK Publishers, 1971. 15 pp.

How to Confess Christ. Netherlands, IRCK, 1971. 16 pp.

The Westminster Confession and Modern Society. Scotland, Scottish Reformed Fellowship, 1972. 20 pp.

Communist Eschatology. U.S.A., Presbyterian and Reformed Pub. Co., 1973. 1201 pp.

Origin and Destiny of Man. U.S.A., Presbyterian and Reformed Pub. Co., 1973. 125 pp.

Can Scholarship be Christian? U.S.A., Christian Studies Center, 1974. 7 pp.

Victory over the Worldly Spirit of This Age. U.S.A., Christian Studies Center, 1974. 8 pp.

Loving God with all our Mind. U.S.A., Christian Studies Center, 1974. 7 pp.

Who Rules History: God or Jehovah? U.S.A., Christian Studies Center, 1974. 7 pp.

Rushdoony's "Institutes of Biblical Law." U.S.A., Presbyterian Journal, 1975.

Sondag die Sabbat. R.S.A., NGK Publishers, 1975. 53 pp.

Ten Commandments Today! England, Lord's Day Observ. Soc. 1976. 20 pp.

The Central Significance of Culture. U.S.A., Presbyterian & Reformed Pub. Co., 1976. 164 pp.

The Christian Manifesto of 1984. U.S.A.: Christan Liberty Press, 1976. 18 pp.

What About Baptism? Scotland, Scottish Reformed Fellowship, 1976. 17 pp.

About Sunday. England: Lord's Day Observance Society, 1978. 78 pp.

Christianity and Culture. U.S.A., Call, 1978.

The Office of All Believers. U.S.A., PCA Commissioners' Handbook, 1978.

The Office of Deacon. U.S.A., PCA Commissioners' Handbook, 1978. 27 pp.

The Ministry of the Word. U.S.A., PCA Commissioners' Handbook, Decatur, Ga., U.S.A., 1978. 55 pp.

The Chief Characters in Scripture. U.S.A., Herald of the Covenant, 1978.

Should the Preacher be the Only Ruling Elder? U.S.A., Herald of the Covenant, 1978.

Christianity on the Death Penalty. U.S.A., Herald of the Covenant, 1979.

Pornography and Censorship. U.S.A., The Counsel of Chalcedon, 1979.

Free Will and Free Grace. U.S.A., The Counsel of Chalcedon, 1979.

Christocracy: The Divine Savior's Law for All Mankind. U.S.A., Jesus Lives, 1979. 25 pp.

Toward a Biblical Theology. U.S.A.: Jesus Lives, 1979. 12 pp.

Effective Evangelism (Forward: Dr. P. Y. De Jong). U.S.A.: J. L., 1979. 12 pp.

Are the Mosaic Laws for Today? U.S.A.: Jesus Lives, 1979. 52 pp.

Creation and Commission. U.S.A.: Jesus Lives, 1979. 40 pp.

Mt. Sinai and the Sermon on the Mount. U.S.A.: Jesus Lives, 1979. 23 pp.

Communism (in Korean). Korean Journal of Reformed Theology, 1980. 25 pp.

Neglecting Your Baby? (in Korean). Korean Journal of Reformed Theology, 1980. 12 pp.

An Interview with Nigel Lee. Australia: *Australian Presbyterian Life*, 1981.

Have You Neglected Your Baby? Australia, *Jesus Lives*, 1981. 13 pp.

Committed to Christ: Called to Change! Australia, *The Presbyter*, 1981.

Gambling and God's Law. Australia, *Australian Presbyterian Life*, Aug. 1981.

Is Predestination Scriptural? Australia, *Australian Presbyterian Life*, Sept. 1981.

John Calvin: True Presbyterian. Australia: *Jesus Lives*, 1981. 22 pp.

Communism: Christian Evaluation. Australia: *Jesus Lives*, 1981. 74 pp.

Abraham Kuyper and the Rebirth of Knowledge. Australia, *Jesus Lives*, 1981. 12 pp.

Will Christ or Satan Win This World? Australia: *Jesus Lives*, 1981. 32 pp.

The Call to the Ministry. Australia, C.T.M., 1982.

The Necessity of Public Recognition of the Sabbath. U.S.A.: Lord's Day Alliance. 1982.

Nec Tamen Consumebatur! U.S.A., *The Counsel of Chalcedon*, Feb. 1982.

The Conquest of Creation. U.S.A., *The Counsel of Chalcedon*, Feb. 1982.

Immanuel's Invincibility. U.S.A., *Counsel of Chalcedon*, Nov. 1982.

Salvation, Sin and Sickness. Australia, *PCQ White Book*, 1983. 19 pp.

Preaching and Evangelising. Australia, *Australian Presbyterian Life*, July 1984.

The Importance of the Family. Australia, *Living Water*, July 1984.

Report on Human Reproduction. Australia, *PCQ White Book*, 1984.

Miracles and Pseudo-Miracles. Australia, *PCQ White Book*, 1985. 8 pp.

May Christians Ever Go to Law? Australia, *FACS Report*, 1985. 7 pp.

Biblical Christianity vs. Unbiblical Pacifism. U.S.A., *The Counsel of Chalcedon*, 1985.

The Importance of the Family. Australia, *PCQ Church Office Bulletin*, 1985.

Communion for Children? U.S.A., *The Counsel of Chalcedon*, 1985. 7 pp.

Leithart vs. Lee & Lee vs. Leithart. U.S.A., *The Counsel of Chalcedon*, 1985.

Reflections: Paedocommunion in the OPC and the PCA. U.S.A., *The Counsel of Chalcedon*.

Pentecostalism: Outpour or Heresy? U.S.A., Commonwealth Publishers, 1986. 79 pp.

Calvin on Creation. South Africa, P.U.C.H.E., 1986. 53 pp.

Revealed to Babies! U.S.A., *Commonwealth Publishers*, 1986. 20 pp.

Who'll Come A-Praising Jehovah with Me? Australia, *Aust. Presb. Living Today*, Mar. 1986.

Battle Hymn of Christ's Church. U.S.A. Fire on the Mountain. 1986.

How to Keep On Being Filled with the Spirit. Australia, COB, 1986.

White South Africa's "Total Depravity"? U.S.A., *Journey*, 1987.

The Severe Limitations of Most "Histories." U.S.A., *Journey*, 1988.

Introduction to Crampton's "Upon This Rock." U.S.A., *Journey*, 1988.

Family Fabric. Australia, *Queensland Theological Hall Magazine*, 1988.

Biblical Private Property vs. Socialism. Australia, *Ex Nihilo Technical Journal*, 1988. 7 pp.

"*Jewish" Creation Story?* Australia, *Australian Presbyterian Living Today*, 1988.

Catechizing Toward Revival! U.S.A., *Journey*, 1988.

Neo-Paganism. Australia, *Australian Presbyterian Living Today*, 1989.

Religion and Culture. U.S.A., *The Counsel of Chalcedon*, 1989.

Glasnost! Australia: *FACS Report*, June 1989.

The Antipaidocommunionistic O.T. Israelites. U.S.A., *Journey*, May 1989.

Conclusion of Communism? U.S.A., *The Bell Ringer*, 1989.

Sprinkling Is Scriptural! England, *The Presbyterian*, 1990. 44 pp.

Biblical Presbyterian Eldership from Genesis to Revelation. England, *The Presbyterian*, 1990.

Abortion, Human Cloning, IVF, and Murder! Australia, *Australian Presbyterian Living Today*, 1990.

Scripture the Final Revelation! England, *The Presbyterian*, 1990. 11 pp.

The Baptism of the Spirit and Dr. Martyn Lloyd-Jones. England, *The Presbyterian*, 1990.

The Ruling Eldership. Australia, *The Reformed Journal*, 1990.

The Office of All Believers. Australia, *The Reformed Journal*, 1990.

Britain's Very Earliest Christianity. Australia, *The Reformed Journal*, 1990.

Zens's "Building Up the Body." England, *The Presbyterian*, 1991. 5 pp.

Lee versus Zens. England, *The Presbyterian*, 1991. 5 pp.

Codling's Non-Cessation of Revelatory Gifts. England, *The Presbyterian*, 1991.

Battle Hymn of the Christian Church. U.S.A., *Fire on Mountain*, 1991.

Biblical Principles for Christian Church Architecture. England, *The Presbyterian*, 1991. 41 pp.

Should Elders and Preachers Ever Rotate? Australia, *The Reformed Journal*, Apr.-May 1991.

Luther on Islam. Australia, *The Reformed Journal*, July–Aug 1991. 6 pp.

The Roots and the Rise of Anabaptist Heretics. Australia, *FACS*, 1991. 8 pp.

The Christian Afrikaners, 1652–1980. South Africa, Gospel Defence League, 1991. 215 pp.

Revive Your Work! (editor). Australia, Presbyterian Church of Queensland, 1991. 104 pp.

Introduction to Revival. Australia, Presbyterian Church of Queensland, 1991.

Keys to Revival. Australia, Presbyterian Church of Queensland, 1991. 7 pp.

Revival and Daily Family Worship. Australia, Presbyterian Church of Queensland, 1991. 10 pp.

Revival through "Prophesying." Australia, Presbyterian Church of Queensland, 1991. 5 pp.

Communism and the Bible. Capetown, South Africa, Gospel Defence League, 1991. 29 pp.

The Complete Book of Psalms for Singing. England, *The Presbyterian*, 1991.

Neglecting Your Baby? England, *The Presbyterian*, 1991, rep. 16 pp.

Praying for Expected Revival. England, *The Presbyterian*, 1991.

Rev. Dr. John Philpot the Protestant. Australia, *The Reformed Journal,* Sep.–Oct. 1991.

From Mary's Romanism to Elizabethan Puritanism. Australia, *The Reformed Journal,* 1992.

God's Gender? Australia, *Australian Presbyterian Living Today,* Jan.–Feb. 1992.

Matthew Henry's Covenantal Home Life. Australia, *The Reformed Journal,* 1992. 7 pp.

Thornwell on Validity of Romish Baptism. England, *The Presbyterian,* 1992.

The Controversy on Australian Women's Ordination. U.S.A.: *Christian Observer,* 1992. 3 pp.

Augustine on the Cessation of Miracles. Australia, *The Reformed Journal,* 1992.

Beza's "The Christian Faith." Australia, *The Reformed Journal,* 1992.

Jewish Law Professor Praises Christianity. Australia, *The Reformed Journal,* 1992.

Antichrist in Scripture. England, *Focus,* 1992. 58 pp.

Culture (in Korean). Korean Society for Reformed Faith and Action, 1992. 208 pp.

PCA Can Refuse Ordination of Women. U.S.A., *Christian Observer,* 1992.

From Atheist to Christian Minister. England, *Focus,* 1992.

The 1992 Litigation against our GAA. Australia: *Presbyterians for Revival,* 1992.

The Electoral Review Commission's Paper No. 20. Australia: *The Reformed Journal,* 1992.

Calvin on the Weekly Sabbath. England: *British Ref. Journ.,* 1993. 17 pp.

Toward a Biblical Philosophy. U.S.A., Persuasive Press, 1993. 60 pp.

Abortion. Australia, *PCQ Church Office Bulletin,* Jan. 1994.

To the Triune God be All the Glory! U.S.A., *The Counsel of Chalcedon,* Jan. 1994.

The Christian Faith. Ulster, *Covenanter Witness,* Jan. 1994.

Principles for Church Discipline. U.S.A., *Presbyterian Witness,* 1994. 5 pp.

Thou Shalt Not Invitrofertilize! Australia, *Backbone,* Jan.–Mar. 1994.

What Sunday's Really All About. Australia, *The Call,* Feb. 1994. 6 pp.

The Workings and the Purposes of Presbytery. U.S.A., *Presbyterian Witness,* 1994.

The Fascinating History of Early Britain. England, *British Reformed Journal,* July 1994. 11 pp.

The Anabaptists and Their Stepchildren. U.S.A., *Blue Banner,* 1994. 62 pp.

My Father's Slayer Saved! Australia, Wilston Presbyterian Church, 1994. 10 pp.

Robber Redeemed! Australia, *Australian Presbyterian Living Today.* Dec. 1995.

Professor Lee Responds to Dr. Westcott. England, *British Reformed Journal,* Jan.–Mar. 1995.

On Common Law. U.S.A., *The Counsel of Chalcedon,* Atlanta, Ga., Mar. & Apr. 1995. 6 pp.

IVF and Euthanasia. Australia, *Australian Presbyterian Living Today,* Sept. 1995.

Lee vs. Jordan on Paedocommunion. U.S.A.: *Blue Banner,* 1995. 10 pp.

Stolen Embryos. Australia: *Australian Presbyterian Living Today,* Jan.–Feb. 1996.

Dr. John Owen Re-Presbyterianized. England, *British Reformed Journal*, 1995-1996. 20 pp.

Arrest Abortionists! Australia, *Australian Presbyterian Living Today*, July 1996.

Patrick and His Writings. U.S.A.: *The Counsel of Chalcedon*, Jul.–Aug. 1996. 10 pp.

Many Errors. Australia, *Australian Presbyterian Living Today*, Jan.–Feb. 1997.

God and Guns. Britain, *Reformed Fellowship News Alert*, March 1997.

An Open Letter to the Australian Prime Minister. Britain, *Reformed Fellowship News Alert*, March 1997.

Brothers Because of Bloodshed. Atlanta, *The Counsel of Chalcedon*, July 1997. 17 pp.

'n Nuwejaarsboodskap. Brisbane, *Die Bostelegraaf.* Jan. 1998.

'n Kersfees vanuit die Buffeljagstronk. Warren NSW, *Die Bostelegraaf.* Jan. 1998.

Twenty-five Theses for a 21st Century Reformation. Brisbane, *FACS Report.* Feb. 1998.

25 Stellings vir 'n 21-eeuse Hervorming. Pretoria, *Esra Verslag.* Apr/Mei 1998.

Thoughts on the Lord's Day. Hampton Va., *The Presbyterian Witness.* Fall 1998.

John's Revelation Unveiled. Pretoria, *Ligstryders.* Nov. 1999. 340 pp.

How My Father's Killer Found Salvation. Prison Fellowship of Queensland, *Unchained*, 2000.

Skrifoordenking n.a.v. Matt. 28:18–20. Pretoria, *Esra Verslag*, April–June, 2000. 4 pp.

Christian Private Property vs. Socialistic Common Property. Grand Rapids: Theological Forum, Reformed Ecumenical Council, May 2000. 13 pp.

Kwartaallikse Nagmaalsviering in Bybelse Jaarseisoene. Pretoria, *Esra Verslag.* 2000. 7 pp.

John's Revelation Unveiled. El Paso, Texas: Historicism Foundation. Dec. 2000. 354 pp.

Daily Family Worship. Signposts: Menlo Park RSA. Dec. 2000. 462 pp.

Tiny Human Life. Ligstryders: Pretoria. 2001. 971 pp.

Many of my lectures appear in the book *Die Christenpad* alias *The Christian Path* (Ligstryders, Pretoria, 2002). 342 pp.

Adventures with God, Bexley Publications, U.K., January 2006.

The Godly Life of John Calvin, Bexley Publications, U.K., January 2006.

King Alfred the Great and Our Common Law, Bexley Publications, U.K., January 2006.

Sixth-Century Christian Britain from King Arthur to Rome's Austin, Bexley Publications, U.K., January 2006.

Always Victorious! The Earliest Church Not Pre- but Postmillennial, Bexley Publications, U.K., January 2006.

"Goldmine Rescues," in *Free Xpression*, West Hoxton NSW, June 2006.

"Andrew Murray: Calvinist or Pentecostalist?" in *New Southern Presbyterian Review*, Sept. 2006.

"King Alfred the Great and our Common Law (Part 1 & 11)," in *The Counsel of Chalcedon*, Cumming, GA, March–April ff., 2007. 9 pp.

God's Ten Commandments: Yesterday, Today, Forever. Dedicated to former Alabama Chief Justice Roy Moore. Ventura, CA: Nordskog Publishing, Inc., 2007. 128 pp.

Concerning God's Law

"Blessed is the man that walks not in the council of the ungodly, nor stands in the way of sinners, nor sits in the seat of the scornful. But his delight is in the law of The Lord; and in His law does he meditate day and night."
The Holy Bible (Psalm 1:1-2)

England (December 24, 1167–October 18, 1216) in the meadow of Runnymeade, under pressure from the English barons. This was the first time the absolute power of a king was limited by law, guaranteeing certain rights to his subjects. Included in the Magna Carta provisions were:

". . . The king himself ought not to be under a man but under God and under the law, because the law makes the king . . . for there is no king where will governs and not law. . . .

"Know ye that we, in the presence of God, and for the salvation of our souls, and the souls of all our ancestors and heirs, and unto the honor of God and the advancement of Holy Church . . . have in the first place granted to God, and by this our present charter confirmed for us and our heirs forever."
Magna Carta (1215)

"For each individual there is some law, some code, some "voice of authority," which sets his values, regulates his conduct, and prescribes his life-system. It is much the same with nations. Each nation has some basic law, some set of code and statute, by which it sets its standards, conducts its affairs and governs its people.

"Thus, we may observe: Man lives by law. The root question is this: 'By what law? By whose law?' His own? Or, Caesar's? Or, God's?

"'Blessed is the nation whose God is The Lord!' We who are His, then, must lead the way. We who have made Christ our King must establish His law in our hearts—and then go forth to restore His law in the nation; empowered by Him, seeking not the applause of men but seeking the approval of The Lord our God. Not hiding for fear of scorn or alienation; not standing mute for fear of ridicule or ostracism—but going forth in His name, raising His banner of truth, Christian soldiers going forth in obedience to His commission and in love for the lost to war against satan and his serpents. This is the task for godly Christians . . . even as we await His return."

Rus Walton ("On Obedience to God's Laws"
Letter from Plymouth Rock Foundation, Plymouth, MA)

"I had always thought that the phrase 'We are not under law, but under grace' taught that we had no obligations to obey God's ethical standards. 'That's the Old Testament' was an easy (but fallacious) way to dismiss the Mosaic Law."

"Theonomy" is derived from a combination of two

Greek words: *theos* ("God") and *nomos* ("law"). It simply means "God's Law." Broadly speaking the term describes the Christian ethical position that holds that God's Word determines what is right and wrong, rather than 'natural law'. More narrowly "theonomy" is generally understood to point out the righteousness and practicality of the Mosaic civil code for modern application.

" . . . When we read the Old Testament Scriptures, we find that God shows a special jealousy and is adamant to maintain that the Law given through Moses is His Law. The Law of Moses is identified over and over as the Law of Jehovah: e.g., Deut. 30:10; Josh. 24:26; 2 Kings 10:31, 17:13, 21:8; 1 Chron. 22:12; 2 Chron. 6:16, 31:21; Ezra 7:6, 12, 14, 21; Neh. 8:8, 18, 9:3, 10:28, 29; Pss. 78:1, 81:4, 89:30, 119:34, 77, 92, 109, 174; Isa. 1:10; Jer. 6:19, 9:13, 16:11, 26:4, 31:33, 44:10, 22:26; Dan. 6:5; Hos. 4:6, 8:1.

"If the Law could not be set aside to spare God's own son, how may we surmise that it will be set aside for the New Covenant era? It is the standard of God's righteousness, the breach of which brings condemnation. The Cross is an eternal testimony to the righteousness of and the continuing validity of God's Law.

"God's Law was in fact designed to be a model for the nations.

"The nations around Israel were often judged for breaching God's moral standards, but never for breaching the Mosaic covenantal form."

Kenneth L. Gentry, Jr. (*God's Law in the Modern World:*
The Continuing Relevance of Old Testament Law.
San Antonio, TX: Vision Forum Ministries, 1993, 9-10)

"It is impossible to rightly govern a nation without God and the Bible."

George Washington
(1732–1799, first president, Father of Our Country)

"Power and the law are not synonymous. In truth they are frequently in opposition and irreconcilable. There is God's Law from which all equitable laws of man emerge and by which men must live if they are not to die in oppression, chaos and despair.

"Divorced from God's eternal and immutable Law, established before the founding of the suns, man's power is evil no matter the noble words with which it is employed or the motives urged when enforcing it. Men of good will, mindful therefore of the Law laid down by God, will oppose government whose rule is by men and, if they wish to survive as a nation, they will destroy that government which attempts to adjudicate by the whim or power of venal judges."

Marcus Tullius Cicero
(Roman, 106 B.C.–43 B.C.)

"The laws of nature are the laws of God, Whose authority can be superseded by no power on earth. A legislature must not obstruct our obedience to Him from Whose punishment they cannot protect us. All human constitutions which contradict His laws, we are in conscience bound to disobey."

George Mason
(1725–1792, founding father)

"The duties of men are summarily comprised in the Ten Commandments, consisting of two tables; one comprehending the duties which we owe immediately to God—the other, the duties we owe to our fellow men."

Noah Webster
(1758–1843, founding father)

"Law is a plan for the future. To return to law which undergirds and establishes a Christian future under God, it is necessary to know God in Christ, and to know His law and to know it well. The future we want is a future under God, not under tyrants. The law we need is a law which protects the Christian man in his God-given liberties rather than a law giving the state god-like powers over man."

"The ground of liberty is Jesus Christ. Biblical faith places authority in the triune God—God the Father, God the Son, and God the Holy Ghost—and in God's inspired and infallible word, the Bible. God does not compete with man as humanistic authorities do. He is above, over, and beyond man. The purpose of His law and of His government is to establish man in godly order and in true liberty. Because God has created this world and history, God does not seek to obliterate history but to bring man and history to fulfilment."

"By means of the state, by civil government, God's righteousness is to be expressed in law, godly law, and the order this law establishes is justice. Take away God's standard of righteousness from the law, and you strip the law of justice and reduce it to anti-law. . . .

"By denying the relevance of God's law to man's law, and by divorcing law from the righteousness of God, humanism has made law the expression of man's logic and experience. God's higher law is denied, and man becomes the ultimate law and law-giver. . . . Moreover, because humanism has no ultimate right or wrong, its law is democratic law, that is, it simply expresses the will of the people. But the will of man, whether as an individual or en masse, is, according to Scripture, a sinful will. Sinful man is not interested in justice; he is interested in himself, in getting more and more of the best for himself."

Dr. Rousas John Rushdoony
(founder, The Chalcedon Foundation. *The Law & Liberty.*
Vallecito, CA: Ross House Books, 1984, 29, 33, 91)

"The answer lies in Christian Reconstruction—the reestablishing of civilization in terms of Biblical law. This is what we mean by 'theocracy.' Yet it is not the rule of a religious elite, but a social order sustained by the faithfulness of self-government."

Mark R. Rushdoony
(president, The Chalcedon Foundation, Vallecito, California, 2007)

"The Ten Commandments...are the sum of the moral law."

John Witherspoon
(1723-1794, president of Princeton, signer of the Declaration of Independence)

"The moral law is that law to which man has been subjected by his Creator."

Thomas Jefferson
(1743-1826, third U.S. president, signer of the Declaration)

"The moral, or natural law, was given by the Sovereign of the universe to all mankind."

John Jay (1745–1829, Chief Justice, co-author of the *Federalist Papers*)

"Now I want to briefly dispel the second misconception that law is not a part of the new covenant. To do this I want to look at Romans 10:4 (NKJ), 'Christ is the end of the law for righteousness to everyone who believes.' It seems that many have taken the wrong definition for 'end' when they interpret the phrase 'Christ is the end of the law' to mean Christ has done away with the law.

"However, the correct meaning is that Christ is the goal or purpose of the law. This is accurately interpreted by the New Jerusalem Bible which says 'the Law has found its fulfillment in Christ so that all who have faith will be justified.'

"If Jesus put an end to our need to obey the moral law, He would have surely taught that. Instead he emphatically stated: 'Do not think that I came to destroy the Law or the Prophets. I did not come to destroy but to fulfill. For assuredly, I say to you, till heaven and earth pass away, one jot or one tittle will by no means pass from the law till all is fulfilled. Whoever therefore breaks one of the least of these commandments, and teaches men so, shall be called least in the kingdom of heaven; but whoever does and teaches them, he shall be called great in the kingdom of heaven. For I say to you, that unless your righteousness exceeds the righteousness of the scribes and Pharisees, you will by no means enter the kingdom of heaven.' (Mt. 5:17–20)"

Vonne L. Fugate (*The Ten Commandments—From Tablets of Stone into the Hearts of God's People.* Omaha, NE: Thy Word Is Truth Publishers, 2005, 5-6)

"Where the Lord of the covenant Himself answers that question—and it was precisely that issue which He was raising (or sensing from His audience)—Biblical theologians are not free to overlook the answer or adopt another one. Indeed, Jesus specifically warned those who are teachers that they come under His displeasure if they tell those who hear them that they may set aside even the least commandment of the Old Testament law (Mt. 5:19). There is no exegetical stalemate or standoff here, as though non-theonomists can adduce equally strong, universal, and pointed statements from Jesus (or the apostles) that every jot and tittle, indeed even the greatest commandment, have been revoked by the advent of the Messiah and the New Covenant. Christ speaking in the Scriptures does not permit silence to revoke the Old Testament law of God."
Greg L. Bahnsen (*No Other Standard—Theonomy and Its Critics.* Tyler, TX: Institute for Christian Economics and I.C.E. FreeBooks, 1991, 71–72)

"The law established by the Creator, which has existed from the beginning, extends over the whole globe, is everywhere and at all times binding upon mankind. This is the law of God by which He makes His way known to man and is paramount to all human control."
Rufus King
(1755–1827, signer of the Constitution, framer of the Bill of Rights)

"If someone came to you and asked, 'What must I do to obtain eternal life?'—how would you respond? Jesus was asked this question at least twice. When a rich young ruler came to Him asking this question Jesus responded by saying: 'You know the commandments,' and then he briefly stated the last six commandments (Mark 10:17–19; Luke 18:18–20).

"When a lawyer asked Jesus this question (Luke 10:25–28), Jesus in turn asked him 'what is written in the Law?' The lawyer responded by quoting from the Law: 'You shall love the Lord your God with all your heart, and with all your soul, and with all your strength, and with all your mind; and your neighbor as yourself.' This was a summary of the Ten commandments. Jesus said to this man, 'You have answered correctly,' and then quoting from the law (Lev. 18:5) stated, 'Do this, and you will live.'

"Jesus is not saying that we earn our salvation by your works or by keeping the law, for salvation is the gift of God and given by His grace. But Jesus is reiterating what all the Bible teaches—that His Law/Word, which is summarized by the Ten Commandments, contains principles that, if obeyed, produce life—life for men and nations—but if ignored, produce death (see Deut. 29).

"God showed His love to mankind by giving us His Law/Word and sending us His Son, a living demonstration of His Word. We in turn show our love to Him by obeying His commands. Jesus said, 'If you love Me, keep my commands.'

"The fruit of Jesus' atonement and of His sending the Holy Spirit to live in us is life for mankind. How is this life produced in us? The Holy Spirit enables redeemed man to do His will and walk in His truth—that is, to follow His commands. His law is now written in our hearts. The Spirit empowers us to keep His commands, which produces life for us on this earth."

Stephen McDowell (*The Ten Commandments & Modern Society.*
Charlottesville, VA: Providence Foundation, 1999, 2000, 1)

"Suppose a nation in some distant region, should take the Bible for their only law book, and every member should regulate his conduct by the precepts there exhibited. . . . What a Utopia—what a Paradise would this region be."

John Adams
(1735–1826, second U.S. president, founding father)

"The laws which regulate our conduct are the laws of man and the laws of God. . . . The sanctions of the Divine law . . . cover the whole area of human action."

Dewitt Clinton
(1769–1828, framer of the Constitution)

"The Ten Commandments were referred to directly by America's founders and leaders as the: Laws of God, Ordinances of God, Statutes of God, Divine Law, Revealed Law, Holy Law, Book of Laws, Eternal Laws, Laws given to Moses on the Mount, His Just and Holy Laws, the Decalogue, Foundation of Our Holy Religion, Immutable Laws of Good and Evil, Government of God, etc. The Ten Commandments were referred to indirectly in statements made in the context of the religion, virtue, principles and morals."

William J. Federer (*The Ten Commandments & their Influence on American Law.* St. Louis, MO: Amerisearch, Inc. 2003, 17)

"The law given from Sinai was a civil and municipal as well as a moral and religious code; it contained many statutes . . . of universal application—laws essential to the existence of men in society, and most of which have been enacted by every nation which ever professed any code of laws. . . . Vain, indeed, would be the search among the writings of profane antiquity . . . to find so broad, so complete and so solid a basis for morality as this Decalogue lays down."

John Quincy Adams
(1767–1848, sixth U.S. president, founding father)

"Human law must rest its authority ultimately upon the authority of that law which is divine. Far from being rivals or enemies, religion and law are twin sisters, friends, and mutual assistants. Indeed these two sciences run into each other."

James Wilson
(1742–1798, Constitutional signer and Supreme Court Justice)

"All societies of men must be governed in some way or other. The less they may have of stringent State Government, the more they must have of individual self-government. The less they rely on public law or physical force, the more they must rely on private moral restraint. Men, in a word, must necessarily be controlled, either by a power within them, or by a power without them; either by the Word of God, or by the strong arm of man; either by the Bible or the bayonet."

Robert C. Winthrop
(1809–1994, descendant of the first governor of Massachusetts Bay Colony)

"God is related to the universe, as Creator and Preserver; the laws by which He created all things are those by which He preserves them."
Charles Louis Joseph de Secondat
(The Baron Montesquieu of France. *L'Esprit des Lois*, 1748; in English, *The Spirit of Laws*)

"Revealed Law. This has given manifold occasion for the interposition of Divine Providence; which in compassion to the frailty, the imperfection, and the blindness of human reason, hath been pleased, at sundry times and in divers manners, to discover and enforce its laws by an immediate and direct revelation. The doctrines thus delivered we call the revealed or divine Law, and they are to be found only in the Holy Scriptures. . . . Upon these two foundations, the law of nature and the law of revelation, depend all human laws; that is to say, no human law should be suffered to contradict it."
Sir William Blackstone (English barrister, 1723-1780.
Blackstone's *Commentaries on the Laws of England*)

"The highest service to which a man may attain on earth is to preach the Law of God."
John Wycliffe
(1320?-1384)

"The first duty of the Gospel preacher is to declare God's Law and show the nature of sin, because it will act as a schoolmaster and bring him to everlasting life which is in Jesus Christ."

". . . we would not see nor realize it (what a distressing and

horrible fall in which we lie), if it were not for the Law, and we would have to remain forever lost, if we were not again helped out of it through Christ. Therefore the Law and the Gospel are given to the end that we may learn to know both how guilty we are and to what we should again return."
Martin Luther
(1483–1546)

"The man who does not know the nature of the Law, cannot know the nature of sin."
John Bunyan
(1628–1688)

"Herein is the Law of God above all other laws, that it is a spiritual law. Other laws may forbid compassing and imagining, which are treason in the heart, but cannot take cognizance thereof, unless there be some overt act; but the Law of God takes notice of the iniquity regarded in the heart, though it go no further."
Matthew Henry
(1662–1714)

"The only way we can know whether we are sinning is by knowing His Moral Law."
Jonathan Edwards
(1703–1758)

"First, then, before you can speak peace to your hearts, you must be made to see, made to feel, made to weep over, made to bewail, your actual transgressions against the Law of God."
George Whitefield
(1714–1770)

"Before I preach love, mercy and grace, I must preach sin, Law and judgment." Wesley later advised a friend, "Preach 90 percent Law and 10 percent grace."

"It remains only to show . . . the uses of the Law. And the first use of it, without question, is to convince the world of sin. By this is the sinner discovered to himself. All his fig-leaves are torn away, and he sees that he is 'wretched and poor and miserable, blind and naked.' The Law flashes conviction on every side. He feels himself a mere sinner. He has nothing to pay. His 'mouth is stopped' and he stands 'guilty before God.' To slay the sinner is then the first use of the Law, to destroy the life and strength wherein he trusts and convince him that he is dead while he lives; not only under the sentence of death, but actually dead to God, void of all spiritual life, dead in trespasses and sins."

John Wesley
(1703-1791)

"Ever more the Law must prepare the way for the Gospel. To overlook this in instructing souls, is almost certain to result in false hope, the introduction of a false standard of Christian experience, and to fill the Church with false converts . . . time will make this plain."

Charles Finney
(1792-1875)

"I do not believe that any man can preach the gospel who does not preach the Law. Lower the Law and you dim the light by which man perceives his guilt; this is a very serious loss to the sinner rather than a gain; for it lessens the likelihood of his conviction and conversion. I say you have deprived the gospel of its ablest auxiliary [its most powerful weapon] when you have set aside the Law. You have taken away from it the schoolmaster that is to bring men to Christ . . . They will never accept grace till they tremble before a just and holy Law. Therefore the Law serves a most necessary purpose, and it must not be removed from its place."

Charles Spurgeon
(1834–1892, called the "Prince of Preachers")

"Ask Paul why [the Law] was given. Here is his answer, 'That every mouth may be stopped, and all the world may become guilty before God' (Romans 3:19). The Law stops every man's mouth. I can always tell a man who is near the kingdom of God; his mouth is stopped. This, then, is why God gives us the Law—to show us ourselves in our true colors. . . ."

"God being a perfect God, had to give a perfect Law, and the Law was given not to save men, but to measure them."

D. L. Moody
(1837–1899)

"A new and more powerful proclamation of that law is perhaps the most pressing need of the hour; men would have little difficulty with the gospel if they had only learned the lesson of the law. . . . So it always is: a low view of law always brings legalism in religion; a high view of law makes a man a seeker after grace. Pray God that the high view may again prevail. . . .

"The gospel does not abrogate God's law, but it makes men love it with all their hearts."

J. Gresham Machen
(1881–1937, *What Is Faith?* pp. 141ff., 192)

"The trouble with people who are not seeking for a Savior, and for salvation, is that they do not understand the nature of sin. It is the peculiar function of the Law to bring such an understanding to a man's mind and conscience. That is why great evangelical preachers 300 years ago in the time of the Puritans, and 200 years ago in the time of Whitefield and others, always engaged in what they called a preliminary 'Law work.'"

Dr. Martyn Lloyd-Jones (1899–1981)

"Unless we see our shortcomings in the light of the Law and holiness of God, we do not see them as sin at all."

J. I. Packer (1926–)

"When analyzing the sources the founding fathers read, studied, cited, and recommended to others, it becomes apparent that a number of basic themes of American republicanism have been combined from a variety of inspirations. Many of these ideas are Christian ideals which became parts of the United States Constitution. . . . And we will notice that these principles are either derived from, or at least compatible with, Christianity and the Bible [EDITOR'S NOTE: Here are 7 of the 15 principles enumerated]:

" 1. A belief in God and His providence, by which He guides and controls the universe and the affairs of mankind.

2. A belief in and respect for revealed religion—that is, a recognition that God has revealed His truth through the Holy Scriptures.

6. A belief that God has established certain physical laws for the operation of the universe, as well as certain moral laws for the governance of mankind.

7. A belief that God has revealed His moral laws to man through the Scriptures (revealed or divine law) and through the law of nature, which is discoverable through human reason and the human conscience.

8. A belief that human law must correspond to the divine law and the law of nature. Human laws which contradict the higher law are invalid, nonbinding, and are to be resisted.

9. A belief that the revealed law and the law of nature form the basis for the law of nations (international law) and that this law of nations includes the right of a nation to defend itself against agressors (just warfare).

10. A belief that the revealed law and the law of nature include natural, God-given unalienable human rights which include life, liberty, and property."

John Eidsmoe
(*Christianity and the Constitution: The Faith of Our Founding Fathers.*
Grand Rapids, MI: Baker Book House, 1987, 72–73)

The Decrees of God Are Immutable:
Change of purpose arises either from the want of wisdom or from the want of power. As God is infinite in wisdom and power, there can be with Him no unforeseen emergency and no inadequacy of means, and nothing can resist the execution of His original intention. To Him,

therefore, the causes of change have no existence. With God there is, as the Scriptures teach, "no variableness, neither shadow of turning" (James 1:17). "The counsel of the Lord standeth for ever, the thoughts of His heart to all generations" (Ps. 33:11).

The uniformity of the laws of nature is a constant revelation of the immutability of God. They are now what they were at the beginning of time, and they are the same in every part of the universe. No less stable are the laws which regulate the operations of the reason and conscience. The whole government of God, as the God of nature and as moral governor, rests on the immutability of His counsels."

Charles Hodge (1797–1878. *Systematic Theology*, Abridged Edition. Grand Rapids, MI: Baker Book House, 1988, 196)

It's time that Christians begin to understand what's at stake. There is a battle going on. In many cases, the fire is coming from within the camp. Millions of Christians say they believe the Bible is the word of God, inerrant and infallible. But when it comes to using the Bible as a blueprint for living, they begin to take out their scissors. You've heard the objections:

+ The Old Testament doesn't apply in the church age.
+ You can't put a non-Christian under Biblical law.
+ Since the Christian is under grace, the law is irrelevant.

These objections are myths. Just try to understand the New Testament without the Old Testament. Paul writes that pastors are to be paid, and he supports this from an obscure verse from the Old Testament: "For the Scripture says, 'You shall not muzzle the ox while he is threshing,' and 'The laborer is worthy of his wages'" (1 Tim. 5:18: cf. Deut. 25:4; Lev. 19:13).

Read what the Bible says about the alien in Israel. The alien was required to keep the law just like the covenant-bound Israelite: "There shall be one standard for you; it shall be for the stranger as well as the native, for I am the Lord your God" (Lev. 24:22: cf. Ex. 12:49). The alien was given "equal protection under the law." Aliens could acquire property and accumulate wealth (Lev. 25:47). They were protected from wrong-doing and treated like the "native" Israelite (Lev. 19:33–34). A native-born Israelite could "not wrong a stranger or oppress him" (Ex. 22:21; 23:9). If the alien was bound to keep the law of God, then the law of God was the standard for protecting him against injustice as well (Deut. 1:16: cf. 24:16; 27:19). John the Baptist saw no restriction attached to him when he confronted King Herod and his adulterous relationship with Herodias, the wife of his brother Philip: "For John had been saying to Herod, 'It is not lawful for you to have your brother's wife'" (Mark 6:18: cf. Ex. 20:14).

At a time when the world is looking for firm ground, Christians should be ready, willing and able to turn people to the Bible as the blueprint by which we can build a Christian civilization.

Gary DeMar and Peter Leithart
(*The Reduction of Christianity: A Biblical Response to Dave Hunt.*
Ft. Worth, TX: Dominion Press, 1988, 331–332)

Compiled by
Gerald Christian Nordskog, Publisher

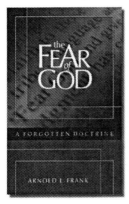

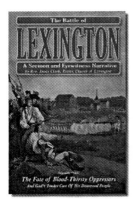

Printed in the United States
96919LV00001B/103-207/A

9 780979 673627